T0294889

Being at Work

Lloyd E. Sandelands

University Press of America,® Inc.
Lanham • Boulder • New York • Toronto • Plymouth, UK

Copyright © 2014 by University Press of America,® Inc.
4501 Forbes Boulevard, Suite 200, Lanham, Maryland 20706
UPA Aquisitions Department (301) 459-3366

10 Thornbury Road, Plymouth PL6 7PP, United Kingdom

Library of Congress Control Number: 2014930073
ISBN: 978-0-7618-6339-7 (paper : alk. paper)—ISBN: 978-0-7618-6340-3 (electronic)

♾️™ The paper used in this publication meets the minimum requirements of American
National Standard for Information Sciences Permanence of Paper for Printed Library
Materials, ANSI/NISO Z39.48-1992.

Contents

Foreword

I am a teacher. And I want to write an honest book about my subject.

I teach business administration; the art of engaging people in commercial enterprise. I teach particularly about the human elements of business—about what people need and desire at work, about how they use their time, talent, and energy for business ends, and about how they can work companionably for a greater good.

What is the truth about people in business? Who can say? I write this book to say what I can. I begin with what I cannot doubt; with the truth of faith. I believe that we are immortal children of God; that we are created in the image and likeness of the One who creates and sustains all being. I begin in the belief that we come into being only as we come into Him.

Sadly I find this truth hard to be honest about. At the university which issues my paycheck, one does not speak of God anywhere, least of all in the classroom. This is not because God is not real and is not the Creator of all being; rather it is because God is too hot to handle—He is regarded by a loud few not as a shining truth, but as an arrogant intolerant idea (often as a mere "idea"!). According to these few, the professor's power to invite students to think is the reason not to seek any truth about God that might trouble a student—and what truth about our Lord, Maker, and Judge would not be trouble in today's "me-first" culture of entitlement? And I admit that for many years this political correctness suited my own "me-first-ness." Had God come up in class (which He never did), I'd have rejected Him as pious opinion, not relevant to a rational scientifically-informed discussion. Not anymore. Over the last number of years, upon returning to the church of my youth and coming into faith for perhaps the first time, I have struggled with the question of God in class, to the point now that I find it impossible to speak wisely about people in business or anywhere else without speaking of

God. To not speak of God is to not speak of the spirit that makes us human. To not speak of God is to not speak of the supreme good of charity in truth. And so in my pedagogical struggle, I began to hedge; I'd ask students in a lesson if there might be an element of the transcendent to consider. Then, seeing my hedge as a cheat, I'd equivocate; I'd point to transcendent aspects of business, what sociologist Peter Berger felicitously called "rumors of angels," and admit my belief in God in asides that were explicitly "off the record." Today, with this book, I hope to come clean, to say plainly that to be wise and good in business, or anywhere else, is to reach for a loving God.

I begin in the subjunctive mood; with "What ifs?" about us at work. *What if* we are more than nature but also being; human being? *What if* we are more than matter and organism but also spirit? *What if* our good reaches beyond this life to eternal life? *What if* we are children of God? *What if* our human being arises and subsists in the One Who is Being itself? What then? *Then* the claims of this book follow in due course. *Then* what makes us human at work—our divine being—is not natural but supernatural, is not for science to say but for faith to reveal. And *then* business is not about "management" (reckoning people as "human resources" to deploy for business ends), but about "ministry" (serving others so they may become the person and community that God created). I argue for a duty of those who lead businesses, a duty of charity in truth, a duty of solemn joy.

In writing this book I have called upon many intellectual heroes. There is Catholic professor of business, Jim Wishloff, who identifies the problem of business life with which I am chiefly concerned. Namely, that "the condition of modernity reveals a mind detached from ultimate reality and a culture without a foundation in what we are;" that the "truth of our being must direct our steps in the economic realm;" and therefore that the "right and proper end of economic enterprise is to serve human well-being in all its dimensions."[1] We are, I agree, detached from reality. We see ourselves, not in the way of faith as spirit or 'being' in God, but in the way of science as objects in part-whole relations to society (and perversely, we think our constructed "world" of objective science "real" while the truth of God's creation a "just so" story told by the pious). And because of this, I agree, we have become strangers to ourselves.

Then there are the modern Catholic popes—Leo the 13th, Pius the 12th, John the 23rd, Paul the 6th, John Paul the 2nd, Benedict the 16th, and now Francis the 1st—in whose encyclical teachings on the Church's social doctrine I see, along with Wishloff, that everyone in business is responsible in everything they do to honor and uphold the human person made in the image of God. I see that business must adhere to the principle of *the common good* (in which the good of the whole person in community is the goal), the principle of *the universal destination of goods* (according to which persons must have access to the well-being necessary for full development), the principle of *subsidiarity* (according to which social institutions must serve the development of persons and never absorb or harm them), the principle of *participation* (according to which persons must be allowed and enabled to contribute to the cultural, economic, political and social life of the community), the principle of *solidarity* (according to which persons are one in being—in dignity and rights—with the community), the principle of *fundamental values* (these being truth, freedom, justice and love), and the principle of the *way of love* (according to which love is recognized as the highest and universal criterion for all ethics).

The modern Popes rely, as do I, on the instruction and inspiration of the metaphysicians of the Church, especially its great Doctor, St. Thomas Aquinas, from whom we all have learned that being human, in business or anywhere else, is being in God. "The human person," writes Aquinas scholar, Jacques Maritain, "is ordained directly to God as its absolute ultimate end. Its direct ordination to God transcends every created common good."[2] The "most essential and dearest aim of Thomism is to make sure that the personal contact of all intellectual creatures with God, as well as their personal subordination to God, be in no way interrupted. Everything else—the whole universe and every social institution—must ultimately minister to this purpose; everything must foster and strengthen and protect the conversation of the soul, every soul, with God."[3] These are heady words and stern marching orders, as the domain of "the whole universe and every social institution" certainly includes the dominant social institution of modern life; business. Thanks to Aquinas I've come to see the flaw in most books about business today; namely, that their authors describe persons, not as we know them to be, but as objects of the sort familiar to a natural or even physical scientist. Their person in business is a thing to measure objectively, study empirically, and explain with causal models. Their person in business is indexed by this or that talent, this or that personality, this or that motivation, and this or that ability to get along with others. What a contrast then to Aquinas who saw persons with a realism that we immediately recognize. He saw persons as we naturally see ourselves, as creative beings—each a play of actuality and potential, each a spirit of unique essence (a soul), and each in search of an ultimate purpose or end; namely, God. His persons are not objects to "see" but are beings to "behold." To know them we must be with them; we must let their stories come alive in us and recognize that we are in-it-together (that their stories are our stories). And thanks to Aquinas' interpreters, Etienne Gilson especially, I've come to see that we cannot know others better than we know ourselves, and that we cannot know ourselves until we know God.[4] Thus, this book about being at work could not be without the metaphysics of St. Thomas, which the Church identifies as a central element of its Magisterium.

And finally there are the social activists and business practitioners who labor in the vineyards of community and business with a faith that lights-up the lives of those in their charge. Among the social activists, I am indebted especially to Peter Maurin and Dorothy Day whose writings about the Catholic Workers Movement teach how the secular ethic of modern capitalism worships mammon instead of God. By making money a greater good than man himself, it puts the banker before butcher, baker, and candlestick maker, as well as before man, wife, child, and God. Its idol, the dollar almighty: "When the banker has the power, the politician has to assure law and order in the profit-making system. When the banker has the power, the educator trains students in the technique of profit making. When the banker has the power, the clergyman is expected to bless the profit-making system or to join the unemployed."[5] And when the dollar is almighty man is enslaved. And among those in business, I am grateful to Tom Chappell, J. Robert Ouimet, Max De Pree, C. William Pollard, Dennis Bakke, and above all Robert Greenleaf who have struggled, each in their own way, against the grain of secular culture to create business organizations that feed the souls of those lucky to work in them.

And in writing this book I have called upon a number of personal heroes. There is my editor Laura Espinoza and the able staff at University Press of America, who with great good cheer helped bring the book into being. There is artist Ricky Romain, whose painting "Alienation" graces the cover of the book, and J'Aimee Cronin of the Artists Rights Society who helped made this painting available. And there are my dear family and friends without whom I would not be. Among these let me thank in particular the late Michael Cohen who commented incisively on crude versions of the early chapters, Monica Worline who took in the whole of the book so that by her sensitive reactions I might better understand what it means, Jim Walsh who gave me new eyes to see key points in a fresh light, and Don Kinder who reminds me that all work and no play makes Lloyd a dull boy. And of course there is my bride, Jane Dutton, on whose constant encouragement I depend to face the world.

My thanks and love to you all.

NOTES

1. Jim Wishloff, "The hard truth of the Easy Essays: The crisis of modernity and the social vision of Peter Maurin," *Journal of Religion and Business Ethics*, Vol. 2: Iss. 2, Article 2, 2011.

2. Jacques Maritain, *The Person and the Common Good*, tr. J.J. Fitzgerald (Notre Dame, IN: University of Notre Dame Press, 1966), p. 15.

3. *Ibid.*

4. Etienne Gilson, *The Spirit of Mediaeval Philosophy*, tr. A.H.C. Downes (Notre Dame, IN: University of Notre Dame Press, 1991), pp. 285-288.

5. Peter Maurin, *Easy Essays* (Eugene, OR: Wipf and Stock, 2010), p. 63.

Chapter One

Being

What is it to be a person, or to be anything else for that matter? To coin a phrase; it all depends on what the meaning of 'is' is.

"Being" is the subject of metaphysics, the branch of philosophy many today call "perennial philosophy," that began with the ancient Greeks—Plato and Aristotle especially—and that reached a peak with the medieval scholastics—Aquinas especially.[1] Aristotle saw that the being or "is-ness" of a thing is a question of its realization. A thing is what it has come to be. And what it is in fact (in actuality, or in Aristotle's terms, in 'act') depends on what it can be (in potentia, or in Aristotle's terms, in 'potency'). Aristotle saw also that the actuality of a thing is given by its four causes. Its *material cause* refers to its matter or substance. Its *formal cause* refers to its form or structure, the way in which its matter or substance is ordered or arranged. Its *efficient cause* refers to that which brings it into being (or, in more technical terms, that which actualizes its potentiality). And its *final cause* refers to its end or purpose (which Aristotle called its "telos"). Aristotle identified the final cause as primary because the other causes are directed to it (matter and form are for a purpose; how something comes to be depends on what it is to be). Thus, according to Aristotle, our human being is to describe by its four causes. We can ask first of our final cause: "What is our purpose; or what are we for?" We can ask of our material and formal causes: "What substance and form enable us to realize our purpose?" And last we can ask of our efficient cause: "How do we realize our purpose and thereby actualize our potency to be?" Finally, Aquinas added to Aristotle's metaphysics the crucial distinction between *what* something is (its *essence*) and *that* it is (its *existence*). After Aristotle, Aquinas saw that real being is always imperfect; about it there is ever a hint of something more, of changes to come, of becoming. As G.K. Chesterton felicitously put it, real being is "less actual than the actuality it

1

implies."[2] Thus, Aquinas saw, there is always a question of existence; always a contingency of whether and how a thing comes to be and of how it subsists through time. Thus, according to Aquinas, our human essence is not simply given, but is ever a possibility that may or may not exist. This contingency, Aquinas saw, points to God.

With no more than this brief on metaphysics we can anticipate a few of the key insights that lie in the pages ahead about what it is to be a human person in business organizations. While it will take a concerted effort over the first three chapters to develop these insights in detail, I list them in promise of what is to come. First, who we are depends on who we can be. Second, who we can be reaches beyond the material and natural to the immaterial and supernatural. Third, we are neither strictly autonomous nor wholly submerged in community; we are at once a person and a communion with others. Fourth, who we are is defined by what we are for (i.e., our final human purpose or end). Fifth, our final purpose or end is to know being itself, which is to know God. And sixth, we can know all of these things by our powers of reason as they are informed by the Revelation of God.

WHO AM I?

Although we do not ordinarily think of ourselves in the highfalutin terms of metaphysical philosophy, we are nevertheless intuitive metaphysicians. We cannot resist the question of being, particularly as it concerns ourselves. To the contrary, most of us most of the time obsess with the question "Who am I?" even though our efforts can only be in vain. And with a stiff drink or three, I myself am only too happy to worry the question to any who would listen and even to those who would not. About this I don't think I am alone.

Among the creatures on earth we stand dramatically apart. Where all living things enjoy certain powers—of inner processes that effect changes of birth, growth, maturation, and death—and where animals are distinguished by their powers of sensation and locomotion (to gain pleasure and to avoid pain)—we alone enjoy the powers of reason and will. We "know" the world and act freely and intelligently upon it. And remarkably, we know that we know and know that we don't know. Thus we alone in creation are aware of possibilities and perfections—not just of being itself but of its qualities of truth, goodness, and beauty. And turning this power on our self, we are aware of our own possibilities and perfections—of freedom, truth, good, personality, and beauty. We know our perfections as "perfections;" as possibilities that we may or may not realize (of potencies we may or may not act out). Recognizing how far we are from perfect, we know, with St. Thomas, that our being is partial and contingent, that there is always the question of how much of it we have.

That we are contingent beings is proof of God. As Aquinas showed, for things to come into or go out of being there must be one that simply is; a being whose essence is existence, a being who creates being from nothing (*creatio ex nihilo*). This absolute and Supreme Being we call God. "The universe," Frank Sheed reminds us, "does not contain within itself the reason for its own existence, so that its existence can be accounted for only by a being who *is* in Himself the sufficient reason for His own existence. God must have made it, and made it as to its totality."[3] What is more, that we know ourselves to be contingent beings means that God created us in His image, with some of His power to know truth, and with some of His love, so that we may know and love Him in a (however faint) likeness of the way He knows and loves us. In a word, we are for Him; for the being that He is. Our hearts, to paraphrase St. Augustine, are restless until they rest in Him. Thus the question "Who are we?" finds its answer in the One who creates and sustains all being. This is the capital "T" Truth of Revelation—the Word of God—without which we cannot begin to know ourselves. As Chesterton points out, reason without faith leads nowhere, except to insanity.[4] "The madman," he says, "is not the man who has lost his reason. The madman is the man who has lost everything except his reason."[5] He lives in a perfectly rounded and closed circle of his own ideas. His world makes complete sense, especially to himself, and he cannot be taken from it. The problem—as the sane among us can see—is that his circle is too small; his "world" is not big enough to function in the wider circle of reality. Revelation, says Chesterton, is the mystery that makes all things clear by putting reason in its place, by insisting upon that wider circle of reality that reason can seek but never truly know. Thus, to see the world in the light of faith is to see it more truly. "Seeing God everywhere and all things upheld by Him," adds Frank Sheed, "is not a matter of sanctity, but of plain sanity, because God *is* everywhere and all things *are* upheld by him. ... To overlook God's presence is not simply to be irreligious; it is a kind of insanity, like overlooking anything else that is actually there."[6]

I AM A CHILD OF GOD

And so let us come to the question "Who am I?" as believers in God, and particularly in the idea shared by the world's three great religions of Abraham—Judaism, Christianity, and Islam—that we are, each of us, a "child of God." And let us take this idea seriously as a revealed truth, without the cynical quotation marks of today's post-modern mood. What does it mean to say: *I am a child of God*?

The declaration—*I am*—marks two metaphysical truths. One is that I am "being," human being. To recall the metaphysics above, this is to assert both an essence—what I am—and an existence—that I am. I am both a way of being and an actuality. And metaphysically speaking, I am a special case. I am more than an object such as a rock or river, whose essence is matter, and I am more than a life such as a daisy or dog, whose essence is organism. I am a spirit whose essence is reason and will—to know reality and to act freely in it. Thus, to say "I am" is to say I am a particular kind of being; a composite of matter, life, and spirit. My matter consists of basic elements—largely carbon, hydrogen, oxygen, and trace minerals—which existed even before the world was formed. My life consists of a particular organization and movement of my matter—a body—that exists for a short time and is constantly subjected to natural causes and contingencies. And my spirit consists of an immaterial capacity for reason and free will bound-up with the absolute and eternal Being of God. This last capacity is a potential of my creation in the image of God. The other metaphysical truth marked by words "I am" is agency and responsibility. While it is with ongoing thanks to God that I exist, it is for me to decide how and therefore who I will be. Granted a free will by God—a will so free that I can, have, and continue to disobey His intentions for me—I am the agent of my being; I decide who I am by what I intend and how I act. This gift of freedom—before which, St. Edith Stein says, "even God pauses"[7] —is the terrible agency of my responsibility: to become the child of God I was created to be.

The prepositional phrase—*child of God*—likewise marks two truths of my human being. One, as just suggested, is that I am the result of God's creative will. My (small "b") being subsists in His (capital "B") Being. Although my mortal body was enacted by my mother and father and ushered into the world by my mother (note the affinity of the words, *mother*, *mater*, and *material*), my immortal spirit was conceived and created by God. My mortal body is the crucible in which my eternal spirit is forged. The other metaphysical truth in the phrase "child of God" is that I am loved by God in something like the way I am/was loved by my parents. The difference (and it is all the difference) is that where my parents' love was partial and imperfect, God's love is whole and perfect. To be created by God, as I am, is by that fact to be good and loved. To be loved by God is to be loved by Love itself.

And not least, even the inconspicuous indefinite article—*a*—has a two-fold metaphysical significance. First, as *a* child of God I am a singularity; a unique being in the intimacy of son-ship or daughter-ship to God, the Creator of all Being. And second, as *a* child of God I am joined with every other person, living or dead, as siblings in the universal human family (His Church). All of us are equally son and daughter of God and thereby equally of infinite dignity and value.

BEING HUMAN IN THE WORLD

What does this teaching of faith—that we are children of God—mean for us today at work? To what truths about our being does it point? Among many, here are six:

We Are Divine

As each of us is a child of God, each of us takes part in His divinity—not only in His being, but also in His virtues of unity, indivisibility, eternity, intelligence, freedom, truth, beauty, and good. These are the possibilities or *potentia* "written into us" by the author of all being. The Christian mystic Thomas Merton referred to our Divine possibilities as "scintilla animae," as the sparks of spirit in which the Absolute recognizes Himself in us.[8] Of this Divinity—this essence of essences, this being of beings—we can acknowledge but cannot speak. As St. Augustine points out, about each of us is the mystery of God, the *mysterium tremendum*. In the fullness with which we incarnate God we become like Christ, who was fully man and fully God. Whereas the being of other creatures is wholly material, wholly natural, and thus wholly mortal, our being is essentially spiritual and in this crucial respect above matter and nature (it is literally "super-natural").

If our true being—the potential being that is our reason to be (that is in Aristotle's terms our "final cause")—is beyond our ken; if our true being is God recognizing Himself in us; then every worldly identity or self we claim for ourselves will be a limitation and lie. And yet how easily and often we make such claims (constantly it seems) and thereby mistake ourselves for something lower than what we are. Without a clear and steady view of the One who is our true and final good, we fashion for ourselves worldly "goods" that are not. We spoil to be rich, we clamber for high position, we aspire for celebrity, and we plead in the mirror to be fairest of all, desperate in the thought that if we could be these things we could be happy. We think that if we *have* more then we could *be* more. This is the precise meaning of sin. If we do not point ourselves to our one, true and final good of God we wander out of being to die a thousand deaths.

Thus, while we are free to live as we will, our being is not our own. We belong to God who creates and sustains all things. As theologian Etienne Gilson put it, every contingent being "owes its contingence to the fact that it only participates being; *it has its being, but it is not its own being*; in the unique sense, that is, in which God is His own being" (emphasis added).[9] Our being, yours and mine, is His ongoing creation. We can be more or less as we live more or less according to His will. And if we live well we can hope to meet God face-to-face and to be joined with the One who is Being itself.

We Are Not for Science to Say

As spiritual beings made in the likeness of God we cannot be described by natural science. As Catholic writer Walker Percy notes, natural science depicts a cosmos that is comprised of only one kind of thing, what he called the "dyadic event":

> It was particles hitting particles, chemical reactions, energy exchanges, gravity attractions between masses, field forces, and so on. As different as such events are, they can all be understood as an interaction of between two or more entities: A⇔B. [10]

As seen by science, organic life is but a special instance of the dyadic logic of the cosmos in which the organism is an "open-system" that is contingently related to its "environment." And as seen by science, man is but a special instance of organism in which reason takes part in the contingent dyadic relationship to the environment. This idea—that man can be conceived like everything else, as an object in space and time—was born in the epoch-making modern philosophy of Rene Descartes. By dividing the immaterial mind (the subject) from the material body (the object), Descartes licensed a scientific materialism focused narrowly on the objective here and how. This materialism could not abide the metaphysical being described by Aristotle and Aquinas, being that exists not only in actuality but also in potency, and it could not abide the being that has material, formal, and final causes in addition to the efficient causes that are the stuff of dyadic events. [11]

And so we find that natural science turns us into something we are not; a *thing* in a world of things. We are *not* a suite of instincts or a plexus of muscle, nerve, and organ, or any material description of biology. We are *not* a social construct or identity; a role or part played in society, a blue, pink, or white-collared worker, a member of a proletariat or bourgeoisie, or any category of sociology. And we are *not* an ego or self comprised of needs, drives, psychodynamics or other elements of psychology. We are other and much more than these sciences can say. We are beings, and beings of a particular kind. We are like the animals in having a body. We, too, are matter in the form of life; a composite of body and soul. But we are unlike the animals in having a spirit beyond the body that is in the image and likeness of God. [12] Like the animals, our material being is subordinate to our organic being. Unlike the animals, our organic being is subordinate to our spiritual being. Thus our human being is to describe uniquely by its spirit. [13]

The futility of the scientific image of man is evident in its confusing twonesses. There is the two-ness of Descartes' mind and body. As mind, we are immaterial subjectivity. As body, we are material objectivity. And, as philosophy since Descartes has learned the hard way, between the two there can be no communication or causality. And there is the two-ness of person and society that has bedeviled social science since the time of Comte, if not before. If our person is a thing—an autonomous "self"—then our society can only be a derivative, a collection of (perhaps) interacting persons. If our society is a thing—an integral whole—then our person can only be a fragment, expression, or manifestation of society (or in anthropologist Leslie White's inimitable telling, an "articulate protoplasmic iron-filing moved by social and cultural magnetic forces").[14] Between these two possibilities go incompatible persons (self vs. iron filing) and incompatible societies (interacting selves vs. an integral whole).

That natural science can only do a poor job with our being, and indeed with every form of being, is a truism. As Pope Benedict XVI points out, we cannot help but be aware of the dimensions, graces, and gifts of being that materialistic science ignores.

> Knowing is not simply a material act, since the object that is known always conceals something beyond the empirical datum. All our knowledge, even the most simple, is always a minor miracle, since it can never be fully explained by the material instruments that we apply to it. In every truth there is something more than we would have expected, in the love we receive there is always an element that surprises us. We should never cease to marvel at these things. In all knowledge and in every act of love the human soul experiences something "over and above," which seems very much like a gift that we receive, or a height to which we are raised.[15]

To account for the spiritual dimension of human being requires "new eyes and a new heart, capable of *rising above a materialistic vision of human events*, capable of glimpsing in the development beyond what technology cannot give."[16] We need "new eyes" to see ourselves in communion with others and with God; to see ourselves as one in being with God. We need "new eyes" to see ourselves, not only on the physical plane of objects in relations of part and whole, but also on the metaphysical plane of being in God. We need to see, to the contrary, that our being is before knowing—that it is before anything we can see or say about ourselves. Who we are and how we relate to one another are not simply or merely opinions or thoughts we have about the world, they are truths and goods of our creation.

We Are in Communion

The presence of God in every person implies that we are neither strictly autonomous nor wholly submerged in community, but to the contrary that we are at once our own person and one in communion with others. To grasp the relation between person and community we can turn to theologian Jacques Maritain's distinction between *animal individuality* and *human personality*.[17] As an individual we exist as an animal exists, as a corporal being. We are a thing among things, a fragment of a species, a part of the collective. As an individual, we relate to community as a part relates to whole. As a personality, in contrast, we exist in self-possession, as a spirit able to contain itself thanks to our intellect and able to super-exist the material world thanks to our freedom. As a personality we are an independent reality which, subsisting spiritually, is a universe unto itself. In contrast to individuality, which is rooted in matter and organism and which is born, develops, and dies with our body, personality is related not to matter and organism but to the deepest and highest dimensions of being, which is God. Says Maritain, our personality is "directly related to the absolute—not in the general way of all creatures, but in a proper way, as the image of God."[18] Personality, therefore, reaches beyond independence and interiority in requiring communication—dialogue—with God first and above all, but also with others who are likewise persons in the image of God. Whereas our individuality is given as a condition of material and organic existence, our personality must be achieved in the knowledge and love of communion. We are more or less of a personality as we participate more or less in the life of God Who is Love. We come into our person only as we come into communion with others—so to say we are a person in communion *and* we are a community of persons. In this we are not part to whole, but whole unto ourselves in the whole of communion. Finally, we must stress that just as we are a composite of body, soul, and spirit, our individuality and personality are not two separate things but part of one reality. As Maritain puts it, "our being is an individual by reason of that in us which is matter and is a person by reason of that in us which is spirit."[19]

There are three points to highlight about our being in communion. First, there is always communion among persons because there is always a commonality in God. As the Bible confirms, whenever two or more are gathered in His name there is love. How much love and how much communion rests with the choices persons make to love God and to love neighbor as self. To be sure, communion is too often interrupted or blocked by selfish individual and/or collective interests and by conflicts that arise among them. Communal being, like personal being, flourishes in the love, play, and fulfillment of reason and dies in sin, as we shall soon see.

Second, our communion is more than an instinctive "animal" form. It is more than a herd, flock, or school; more than a centripetal massing of bodies in which each relinquishes its independence to become part of the whole. While we do sometimes huddle as animals—for example in the familiar and sometimes terrifying masses of an angry street mob or rabid stadium crowd on a Saturday afternoon—these are not truly human communities. "The human community," according to Pope Benedict XVI, "does not absorb the individual, annihilating his autonomy, as happens in various forms of totalitarianism, but rather values him all the more because the relation between individual and community is a relation between one totality and another. ...

The unity of the human family does not submerge the identities of individuals, peoples, and cultures, but makes them more transparent to each other and links them more closely in their legitimate diversity."[20] In this respect our communion is like that of the Triune God. Our persons are unique as the three Divine Persons (of Father, Son, and Holy Spirit) are unique. And our persons are one being as the three Divine Persons are one God. In short, and it is no accident, we are one in love as God is one in love. Thus, although we may speak of our person singly, we must not, as Thomas Merton says, "forget the dimension of relatedness to others. True freedom is openness, availability, the capacity for gift."[21] Poet John Donne spoke well to say "no man is an island." To speak of persons is not to speak of separable beings, but of incarnations of the human being that is of God who is all being. "As a spiritual being," says Pope Benedict XVI, "the human creature is defined through interpersonal relations. The more authentically he or she lives those relations, the more his or her own personal identity matures. It is not by isolation that man establishes his worth, but by placing himself in relations with others and with God."[22]

And finally, whereas our communion is good for all, it is not a coincidence or mutuality of personal goods. It is a mistake to suppose that community is the result of persons pursuing self-interests—an idea attributed to the 18th century economist Adam Smith. Community must answer the greatest good which, as St. Thomas Aquinas made clear, is the beatific vision—is to see God face to face. For Aquinas there can be no common good that does not serve this greatest good. According to Thomist philosopher Jacque Maritain, Aquinas' reasoning runs something as follows:

> The beatific vision, good so personal, knowledge so incommunicable, that the soul of the blessed cannot even express it to itself in an interior word, is the most perfect, the most secret and most divine solitude with God.
>
> Yet it is the most open, most generous and most inhabited solitude. Because of it another society is formed—the society of the multitude of blessed souls, each of which on its own account beholds the divine essence and enjoys the same uncreated Good. They love mutually in God. The uncreated common Good, in which they all participate, constitutes the common good of the celestial city in which they are congregated.[23]

We Are Male and Female in One Flesh

Our first and most important communion—first and most important because all others are built upon it—is the spiritual union of man and woman. "In the beginning," reveals *Genesis*, "… God created man in his *own* image, in the image of God he created him; male and female he created him."[24] By defining Adam and Eve as male and female "in one flesh," Revelation identifies the nuptial union as the purest realization of Being of God.

The spiritual union of male and female in God is significant on two levels. The first and deeper is that it explains how man, alone in creation, is the bridge between the two forms of being created by God, matter and spirit. Where these forms seem to be incommensurate (the one a mortal material substance and the other an immortal immaterial essence) they meet in the nuptial union which "spiritualizes" the body by forming its complementary male and female elements to the image of the eternal God. This is why sex for us can never be a casual affair; it whispers eternity.[25] Considered in its full and true humanness, which is spiritual as well as bodily, sex is a kind of prayer, a bodily contemplation of God.

The second level of significance of the spiritual union of male and female in God is how it engenders communions of every kind. Almost fifty years ago, psychiatrist Karl Stern made the profound remark that "all [human] being is nuptial," meaning that it is a polarity of male and female.[26] For yours truly, this idea that human life is nuptial in its essence resonates as none other because it suggests that nuptial union must be the starting and ending point—the alpha and omega—in the analysis of everything human, including business. As Revelation teaches, sex is the primary potency of our communal life because it is the one and only ordering principle of human society ordained by God. As a noun, sex is the potential division and distinction between male and female. And as a verb, sex is the potential unity of male and female in the image of God. In today's sexually unmoored moral and political culture it is important to emphasize the word "potential" in these definitions of sexual division and unity because the male and female to which they refer are possibilities never fully realized, forms that actual human persons never bring fully into being (as Adam and Eve themselves did not).[27] Human communion is guaranteed, not by the complementary bodies of men and women (bodies that are linked by evolution to those of other animals and that can and do reinforce our communion with sexual pleasure), nor again by the less clear cut and hence less obviously complementary attitudes and inclinations of men and women in society (less clear cut especially to those who understand sexual "equality" to mean "sameness" in all things), but by the union in spirit of Man and Woman in the image and likeness of God. This sets our communions apart from the incidental gatherings of every other creature "that creepeth on the earth." Whatever their outward forms—of family, tribe, nation, race, interest group, association, club, or corporation—our communions bear the indelible stamp of our creation by God in His nuptial image.

Because it is rooted in the nuptial pair, our human communion is like our person in being the image and likeness of God. It is likewise a composite of matter, organism, and spirit. In it there is matter—a mass of persons; organism—an animal association of persons who move together in time and space as birds flock or fish school; and spirit—a supernatural union in God through which persons come to be in the love and play of community. Indeed, our uniquely human tie to God changes everything (the metaphysical step from matter to organism is small compared to that from organism to spirit). When we are open to God we feel, think, and act differently; not as autonomous individuals, but as collaborators in divine oneness. Together we enter realms of spirit, play, art, beauty, truth, and wonder that are before and beyond the material and natural worlds. In these Divine realms, we are the image and likeness of God in the one flesh of male and female.

We Are Contingent

As Aquinas pointed out, our human being is not given once and for all, but is contingent. We come into and go out of being by what we do; by the choices we make and by the actions we take. Being is the fruit of becoming. To be a person is to be of God Who is source and sustainer of all being. This is our greatest good. We come into being by knowing and loving; by knowing and loving God above all, by knowing and loving our neighbor and self, and by knowing and loving all things of God's creation. These latter are instances of the first as neighbor and self are creations in the likeness of God and all other things are creations that bear the imprint of God. We are in and with God, others, and all things. As theologian Maritain points out, the beatific vision, in which we come face to face with God, is the "supremely personal act by which the soul, transcending absolutely every sort of created common good, enters into the very bliss of God."[28]

Thus it is our human fate to be responsible for our being. It is up to us to do the necessary knowing and loving. In the freedom given us by God we bring ourselves into or out of being by accepting or rejecting His truth and good. Virtue is to come into the truth and good of being by acts of faith, prudence, justice, friendship, temperance, and courage. It is the measure of our being, not only of "who" we are but of "whether" and "how much" we are. Vice is to sacrifice the truth and good of being by acts of faithlessness, imprudence, injustice, hate, intemperance, and cowardice. It is the measure of our want of being. And so, when the perennial philosophers declare our greatest good to be God, they wisely mark every other good as secondary and as "good" only as it respects and supports the good of God. When goods not God—such as wealth, power, fame, beauty, safety, esteem, or self-actualization—are taken to be supreme, we come to ruin and unhappiness. While this lesson is perhaps well-known, it seems to require constant rediscovery and reaffirmation.

We Are Each unto Ourselves

Finally, we are never a generic human being, but always *this one* human being. Each of us is *sui generis*; always and everywhere particular; unique in creation. Metaphysicians call this the *principle of identity*; which is that every being is what it is.[29] As a human being we exist not only as an instance of a kind—of a biological species, *Homo sapiens*—with the physical and material qualities proper to it, but also as an absolutely unique spirit. Again, as a spirit in the image of God, we are, like He is, beyond space and time. As our spirit does not take place in space it is integral; it cannot have parts (although it can and does have male and female aspects, as we've seen). And as our spirit does not take place in time it is eternal; it cannot have an end.

Thomas Merton spoke of our integral being as "not simply the Aristotelian essential form but the mature personal identity; ...the "self" that is found after other partial and exterior selves have been discarded as masks."[30] This identity is, again, "that *scintilla animae*, that 'apex' or 'spark' which is a freedom beyond freedom, an identity beyond essence, a self beyond all ego, a being beyond the created realm, and a consciousness that transcends all division, all separation."[31] This, again, is our true being, the Absolute recognizing Himself in us. And thus, says Thomas Aquinas, the good of our person, who is made in the image and likeness of God, is worth more than the good of the whole universe of nature.[32] To this, adds Jacques Maritain, "the free act of the human person, considered in its pure and secret intimacy as a free act, is not of this world. By its liberty, the human person transcends the stars and all the world of nature."[33]

Although we may not ordinarily be aware of God at the center of our being, we have flashes of Him in moments of conscience. As the Second Vatican Council affirmed:

> In the depths of his conscience man detects a law which he does not impose on himself but which holds him to obedience...For man has in his heart a law written by God...Conscience is the most secret core and sanctuary of man. There he is alone with God whose voice echoes in his depths. In a wonderful manner conscience reveals that law which is fulfilled by love of God and neighbor.[34]

The law inscribed by God on our being proves our inalienable dignity. It is also why we should love and respect other persons as we love and respect ourselves. As we are each a child of God we are thereby a brother or sister to one another.

A LOOK BACK AND AHEAD

We look back upon metaphysical first principles; basic ideas about who we are and about what it is to be human. Chief among these, Aristotle gave us the idea of *"essence"* or is-ness. Our human essence, he noted, is our capacity for reason. This essence, he added, is partly realized—in actuality—and partly unrealized—in potency. Aristotle gave us also the means to describe our human being by the typology of four causes—material, formal, efficient, and final. Standing on Aristotle's tall broad shoulders, Aquinas gave us the crucial distinction between *essence* and *existence*, noting that of our being we can ask not only *what* it is, but *whether* it is. By calling attention to the contingency of being, to the fact that what is might not have been, Aquinas led us certainly to a Supreme Being—to God—in Whom essence and existence are one and in Whom all being participates. Taking Aristotle and Aquinas together we came to six conclusions about who we are; namely, we are divine, we are not for science to say, we are in communion, we are male and female in "one flesh," we are contingent, and we are each unto ourselves.

We look ahead to the developments of the next chapters. Chapters 2 and 3 elaborate key philosophical points needed to think clearly and well about people in business. Chapter 2 delves into the special human capacity for reason. It finds this capacity to be a potency of our nuptial being—of our unique spiritual union of man and woman in the image of God. It observes that this capacity is jeopardized by a culture today that is less impressed by and committed to this spiritual union. Chapter 3 considers the moral problem of being a human person. On one hand it finds the human person depleted by a modern world unbalanced by delusions of objectivity and subjectivity. On the other hand it finds the human person ever nourished by the beatitudes described by Jesus Christ in his *Sermon on the Mount*. At long last, Chapters 4 and 5 build upon the first three chapters to look more directly at people in business. Chapter 4 speaks of the ache of work. It identifies some of the key ways business organizations deny the personhood of their members by keeping them from God. Chapter 5 offers hope of a better tomorrow in which business organizations honor and serve the human person. Specifically, it speaks to business leaders of the idea of servant leadership proposed by Robert Greenleaf and of the experiences of five prominent business leaders who have made such leadership real in their organizations. The book culminates in three pieces of advice for would-be leaders of business.

NOTES

1. John W. Carlson, *Understanding our Being* (Washington, D.C.: Catholic University Press, 2008).

2. G.K. Chesterton, *Saint Thomas Aquinas: "The Dumb Ox"* (New York: Doubleday, 1966), p. 144.

3. Frank Sheed, *Theology and Sanity* (San Francisco: Ignatius, 1993), p. 149.

4. G.K. Chesterton, *Orthodoxy* (New York: Image Books, 1959), pp. 7-24.

5. *Ibid*, p. 13.

6. Sheed, *Theology and Sanity*, p. 25.

7. St. Edith Stein, quoted in Pierre-Marie Emonet, O.P., *The Greatest Marvel of Nature*. Translated by Robert R. Barr (New York: Crossroad, 2000).

8. Thomas Merton, *Love and Living* (San Diego, CA: Harvest, 1979).

9. Etienne Gilson, *Spirit of Mediaeval Philosophy*, tr. by A.H.C. Downes (Notre Dame, IN: University of Notre Dame, 1991), p. 90.

10. Walker Percy, *Lost in the Cosmos* (New York: Farrar, Straus & Giroux, 1983), pp. 85-86.

11. While this material causality superficially resembles Aristotle's efficient causality, it is the brainchild of Scottish philosopher David Hume and is actually quite different. Whereas efficient causality for Aristotle was the "how" by which a potency of form is actualized, efficient causality for Hume was a conjunction of events that we experience and call cause and effect but that we cannot rationally justify.

12. We, alone in creation, are a composite of matter, life, and spirit. We are not pure spirit as Gnosticism would have it and we are not pure materiality as scientific materialism would have it. The danger in Gnosticism, as recognized by the Church, is that posed today by so-called "New Age" spirituality. This is to view matter as inimical to spirit and to view the universe as a depravation of God. This is to view God and our own spirit as being out of this world, beyond it. Therefore we are not God incarnate and our body is not essential to our being. The danger in scientific materialism is that it cannot recognize what makes us human. Yes there is a biological continuity between animal and man that can be explained reasonably by evolution, but there is also a metaphysical gulf between animal and man that cannot be explained reasonably by evolution. As novelist Walker Percy puts it; between us and the chimpanzee is a difference greater than between the chimpanzee and the planet Saturn. The peril in materialism has been recognized by the Church as that posed by the "contemporary technological mindset" in which the distinctively human is lost. There is a tendency, she says:

... to consider the problems and emotions of the interior life from a purely psychological point of view, even to the point of neurological reductionism. In this way man's interiority is emptied of its meaning and gradually our awareness of the human soul's ontological depths, as probed by the saints, is lost (Carlson, *Understanding our Being*, p. 76).

This technological mindset, in which man takes his being and development unto himself without acknowledgement of God, is doomed to an empty failure. According to Benedict XVI, this is because the human person is a

...unity of body and soul born of God's creative love and destined for eternal life. The human being develops when he grows in the spirit, when his soul comes to know itself and the truths that God has implanted deep within, when he enters into dialogue with himself and his Creator (Benedict XVI, *Caritas in Veritate*, Encyclical letter delivered July 29, 2009, #21, p. 76).

13. As philosopher Edward Feser observes in *The Last Superstition* (South Bend, IN: St. Augustine's Press, 2008), the scientific materialism that prevails today does so, not as a partiality accepted for the sake of scientific progress, but as an ideology embraced to avoid the moral truths that follow from formal and final causes. If there be a final human good, then we must answer it. We must accept that whatever promotes that final good is also good and that whatever retards that final good is an evil. But to do this would condemn a great many of today's secular values and practices as positive evils.

14. Leslie White, "Culturological vs. psychological interpretations of human behavior," *American Sociological Review, 12*: 686-698, 1948.

15. Pope Benedict XVI, *Caritas in Veritate*, www.vatican.va/holy_father/benedict_xvi/encyclicals, #77.

16. *Ibid*.

17. Jacques Maritain, *The Person and the Common Good* (trans. John J. Fitzgerald) (Notre Dame, IN: University of Notre Dame Press, 1966).

18. *Ibid*, p. 42.

19. *Ibid*, p. 43.

20. Benedict, #53.

21. Merton, *Love and Living*, p. 8.

22. Benedict XVI, *Caritas in Veritate*, #53.

23. Jacques Maritain, *The Person and the Common Good* (Notre Dame, IN: University of Notre Dame Press), pp. 22-24.

24. *Genesis* 1.27.

25. This is why today, despite the so-called "sexual revolution," men and women can't quite accept the idea of a meaningless "hook-up." In such encounters there are still misgivings of uneasy conscience. Notwithstanding our crazy ideas of sexual "liberation," it seems that God will not let sex be less than what he created to be, a realization of His being in our lives that we would feel better welcoming than shunning in shame.

26. Karl Stern, *The Flight from Woman* (St. Paul, MN: Paragon House, 1965), p. 41.

27. It should perhaps not need saying that actual men and women have bodies and live lives that, even at their best, only approximate the Godly ideal of nuptial union. We speak figuratively of a partner as our "better half" or even as our "soul mate" but who can honestly claim to living the truth that we are made for and suffice for one another? As everyone has always known, and the notorious Kinsey Reports documented scientifically decades ago, our actual romances and sexual impulses run roughshod over this ideal, in every possible way.

28. Maritain, p. 21.

29. Carlson, p. 84.

30. Thomas Merton, *Love and Living*, N.B. Burton Stone & Brother P. Hart (eds.) (San Diego: Harvest, 1979), p. 4.

31. *Ibid*, p. 9.

32. Thomas Aquinas, *Summa Theologica*, I, 93, 2.

33. Maritain, *Person and the Common Good*, p. 20.

34. Quoted in Dorothy Day, *Selected Writings*, ed. By R. Ellsberg (Maryknoll, NY: Orbis Books), p. 343.

Chapter Two

In God's Image

How can we be all we can be? How can we become fully human as a person in communion with others? These are the aching questions of life to answer at work and everywhere else.

In the last chapter we identified reason as the thing that makes us human. In this chapter we try to say what this means. We begin by asking "What is reason?" We find that it is our capacity to know what is real. We then ask "What is reason for?" We find that it is to know God by His creation. And finally we ask "How does reason happen?" We find that it happens only as we are the image and likeness of God as "male and female in one flesh."

WHAT IS REASON?

The *American Heritage Dictionary* defines reason as the "capacity for rational thought, inference or discrimination" as well as the use of this capacity "to think logically or to talk or argue logically and persuasively." But this definition does not encompass all that our metaphysicians Aristotle and Aquinas intended by the term. They had a bigger idea of it; an idea as big as human being itself. They conceived of reason broadly as the capacity for consciousness—the capacity that includes inference and logic, but also feeling, intuition, and practical understanding. And they conceived of reason not as a human acquisition or possession but as a property of human being itself. Reason is what makes us human.

Reason is "rational"—that is, it makes sense—not because of anything we bring to it, but because being itself is rational. "Rationality," C.S. Lewis observes, is not something we create, but something we may or may not fully or correctly discern. We receive and respond to a universe that is rife with it:

Where thought is strictly rational it must be, in some odd sense, not ours, but cosmic or super-cosmic. It must be something not shut up inside our heads but already 'out there'—in the universe or behind the universe: either as objective as material Nature or more objective still. Unless all that we take to be knowledge is an illusion, we must hold that in thinking we are not reading rationality into an irrational universe but responding to a rationality with which the universe has always been saturated.[1]

In Lewis we come to the realist truth that the world exists before and apart from us, and in particular that it exists before and apart from our thinking about it. On this view, it's not that the world is rational because we think it is (as philosophers after Descartes, Hume, and Kant argue), rather it's that we think the world is rational because it is. Thus it should not surprise us that the cosmos obeys laws of physics or follows mathematical formulae (though we should be grateful that it does), for these are not our laws or our formulae; we did not create them for the cosmos but discovered them in the cosmos. What we think of as our rational mind is the cosmic and (let's just say it) 'Divine' mind that we barely glimpse as through a glass darkly.

WHAT IS REASON FOR?

To this question our metaphysicians Aristotle and Aquinas answer simply that reason is for knowing being. They could see, as we today often cannot, that the faculty of reason that defines us as human has a natural end and a final cause—namely, to attain truth (we today debate whether there is such a thing). They could see, as we today often cannot, that our will is to act according to the truth discovered by reason (we today think our will is to act according to what we want). And Aquinas could see, as Aristotle could not and as we today often cannot, that the truth and good at reason's end is God. For Aquinas, if the truth is realized most fully as reason reaches most fully to the being of things, and if the good is realized most fully as the will fulfills the truth, then the highest fulfillment of reason must be to know the creator and source of all being—namely, God—and then the highest fulfillment of will must be to serve the One who is Being itself. Aquinas saw that in these two ways—of reason and will—we become the image of God that we are created to be.[2]

This true end of reason is illuminated by the difference between *seeing* and *beholding*. To "see" is to know and master a world of objects by a subject self. In this view, which is the idealism of Descartes, the mind is the faculty which brings all things into existence, the self included—in Descartes infamous phrase, "I think, therefore I am." And in this view, which is the dualism of Descartes, the mind stands apart from and above the world of objects, and indeed apart from and above even the body (which is another object in the world). It is for the mind to pronounce the existence, movement, and interactions of things, ideally with mathematical precision. In contrast, to "behold" is to literally "hold in being." It is to take the being of things into one's own and to be conformed to them. To behold is, so to speak, to become the beheld (by sympathy with its form). It is to understand; literally to "stand-under" or with it.

This distinction between physical "seeing" and metaphysical "beholding" recalls that drawn by theologian Martin Buber between the attitude of mind that conceives objects in time and space—what he called the "I-It" attitude—and the attitude of mind that knows being—what he called the "I-Thou" attitude.[3] To take an ordinary example, one employed by Buber himself, we can encounter a tree, such as the majestic oak outside my office window. On one hand we can see it as a physical structure of root, trunk, branch, and leaf or perhaps more technically as a physical-bio-chemical dynamism of respiration, ATP cycles, and photosynthesis. To this tree we stand in physical relations of time and space. On the other hand we can behold the tree as a being having an essence and purpose. To this tree we stand in metaphysical relation, not as a subject to an object (not as an I to an It), but as a co-being in God who is being itself (as I and Thou). And as with the tree even more with persons, not only others but also ourselves. They and we are not individual bodies only (objects to our subject only) but are more truly personalities alive with being, integral in form, intrinsically good, and beautiful to behold. Across the board, we must be impressed with the profound difference between seeing and beholding. To see is to declare a thing a discrete object apart from our self. To behold is to hold a thing in being with our own.

With the distinction between seeing and beholding we are reminded that every being must remain at least somewhat of a mystery to us. We cannot fully or finally know any being because we cannot fully or finally become that being. With psychologist Owen Barfield, we are reminded to "save the appearances" of things by remembering that they are not the things themselves.[4] This is more than a negative lesson to be humble about what we claim to know (to remember that our perceptions are just that, our perceptions); it is more importantly a positive lesson to be open to possibility. It is to know of all things that they have potentials not yet realized, being not yet become, and truth not yet manifest.

Finally, there is the difference that makes all the difference. In beholding, but not in seeing, we are formed—literally, "in"-formed—by what we know. As we come to know the being of things, we come into being ourselves. And most important of all, we come into God, who is Being itself. This, again, is what we are for; our true desire is not to "see" things apart from ourselves, but to "behold" them by taking them into ourselves, to be thereby enlarged, and to be thereby a more perfect and complete image of God.

HOW DOES REASON HAPPEN?

Having considered what reason is for—which is to know being and thereby God; it is left to consider "how" reason happens—how we are able to know being and thereby God. Or, to put it in the terms of Aristotle's metaphysics; having considered the *final* cause of reason, it is left to consider the *material*, *formal*, and *efficient* causes of reason.

As the historian of philosophy Etienne Gilson has observed, although the one best answer to the question of how we know was provided by Aquinas in the Middle Ages, our modern answer to this question owes largely to Descartes who, after identifying the elements of knowing, muddied our understanding of them by locating bodily sensations and conscious ideas on opposite sides of an abyss. In his *Sixth Meditation* Descartes writes:

> I find in myself a certain passive faculty for feeling (that is to say for receiving and knowing) ideas of sensory things. But it would be useless to me and I could in no way employ it, if there were not in myself or in other beings a separate and active faculty capable of forming and producing these ideas.[5]

While he recognized the existence of what the mind knows, by awarding to the intellect alone the franchise of creating ideas of things and relations (his master image was of a mathematical ideal on the model of Plato's geometry), Descartes overwhelmed philosophy with the puzzle of how ideas and existences are related. That his dualism cannot be correct, and that we should not abide by it, is proved by the mayhem it has loosed. On one hand, it led philosophy to a critical idealism that exempts knowledge from philosophical criticism. Thus David Hume could find that our knowledge of cause and effect has no rational basis. And thus Immanuel Kant could find instead that our knowledge of cause and effect pre-exists in the mind (as an "apriori synthetic"). On the other hand, this dualism reduced philosophy to a scientism which surrenders truth to method. Truth is not what is, but is what science says. Descartes' sundering of idea and existence has been a fateful break, like that suffered by the fairy-tale Humpty-Dumpty, which all of the king's horses and all of the king's men have not been able to put back together again.

But what is true in Descartes, and what we want to hold onto, is his formulation of reason as consisting of two aspects—a passive aspect of sensation which receives and feels and an active aspect of intellect which catalogues and projects. These aspects need not be opposite sides of an abysmal divide of body and mind, but can instead be opposite sides of a single coin of reason. These aspects, let me now suggest, are just those of nuptial being described in chapter 1; they are complementary male and female elements of the human image of God. The nuptial image, which is occasionally realized as a congress of male and female bodies, is in essence a union of male and female in spirit. As we will see below, this spiritual union—which is potential in every person—integrates idea and existence, thought and feeling, and conception and sensation.

Material Cause of Reason

The material cause of reason is at once a story of evolutionary continuity, in which we conserve a mammalian and primate body and soul, and a story of evolutionary discontinuity, in which we take leave of these to establish a spirit uniquely our own. It is the story of our creation in the image of God, a story to tell in the actualities of the nuptial union of male and female.[6] One actuality of nuptial union consists of three elements of sexual concern and behavior—female care of young, male competition for females, and female mate choice—that have been conserved through tens of millions of years of mammalian evolution. This is the first order of species life that at once divides the sexes as to tasks and unites the sexes in the imperative to reproduce.[7] This first mutuality of male and female is a basis of social life throughout the mammalian order. In this we do as other animals do.

A more complex actuality of nuptial union consists of two distinctively human adaptations of species life. One was same-sex grouping: in which men form groups with men and women form groups with women. Although true of men and women alike, same-sex grouping has figured differently in the lives of each. For men, the group enabled hunting on the savannah by coordinating efforts to stalk, mob, and overcome the big game needed to feed and clothe the community. For women, the group facilitated sharing of food and other resources (including defense) in care of children. The second and related human adaptation of social life was the family: that reproducing cell of our kind that consists of a woman with children attached more or less exclusively to a man.[8] Family adapted our kind to conditions where men in groups left the village to hunt and to explore and women stayed closer to home to gather nearby foods and to care for children. Family promised woman a man to return with food, to defend her and her children from attack, and to help with child-care. And family promised man a woman with whom he could mate and from whom he could receive comfort.[9] Thus, in this secondary mutuality of male and female in same-sex groups and family we again find that each element creates and meets the need of the other.[10]

Finally, the most surprising and surpassing actuality of nuptial union is reason or "mind." In this actuality particularly and especially we fulfill our being the image of God. Where the actualities of female care of young, female mate choice, male contest, same sex grouping, and family are universals rooted in the body, the actuality of mind is rooted in the spirit. Mind is the actuality made possible by uniting male and female in spirit in the image of God.[11] The mind, which is not material and is not in time and space, transcends and extends the body, which is material and is in time and space. As psychoanalyst Karl Stern observes, the sexual companionability of the nuptial bond that is obvious in the body reaches to the whole of our being:

> The polarity of the sexes is based on body-build and organ function but not confined to it. The male principle enables us to master our relationship with reality, to solve our problems rationally. Woman acts and reacts out of the dark mysterious depths of the unconscious; i.e. affectively, intuitively. This is no judgment of value but a statement of fact.[12]

Thus our creation as male and female in God's image established the spiritual being we call human. To be human is not only to stand with animals in evolutionary continuity; it is also to stand apart from animals in divine splendor. The actualities of mammalian sexual order (of female care of young, female mate choice, and male contest) prepared the ground for the actualities of human society (of same-sex groups and family) which prepared the ground for the actuality of mind that distinguishes us as the image of God's creative being. Our human being realizes in a unique way the potencies of male and female inherent in our creation by God in His nuptial image. It would be very hard indeed to overstate the gulf this third and last element of sexual order opens between animal and human being.

Formal Cause of Reason

To be sure, the formal cause of reason—of consciousness broadly speaking, including intuition, feeling, and idea—has perplexed even the most acute modern philosophers who speak of it searchingly, if not enigmatically. Ernst Cassirer wrote of "mythic conception," Charles Pierce of "abduction," Jacques Maritain of "connatural knowledge," and Suzanne Langer of "presentational symbolism." As Cassirer described, mind emerges somehow out of the shadows, as a progressive objectification and articulation:

> As soon as the spark has jumped across, as soon as the tension and emotion of the moment has found its discharge in the word or mythical image, a sort of turning point has occurred in human mentality: the inner excitement which was a mere subjective state has vanished, and has been resolved into the objective form of myth or of speech. And now an ever-progressive objectification can begin.[13]

The question for Cassirer, and for philosophers since, has been what is this "spark" that has "jumped across"? What polarity supplies the energy for such a spark and what structure offers the contact points for its arc? While reason's formal cause remains a mystery, we can hark back to Aquinas and the scholastics to suggest a path forward. When lost in shadows we do best to turn to the light. And in reason's shadows there is the light of Revelation. Might the mythic, abducted, connatural, and presentational form of reason be just that proclaimed in Scripture; namely, that of male and female united in the spiritual image of God? Might the nuptial image supply the elements and order of mind? As Cassirer notes, all conception and judgment:

> ...aims at overcoming the illusion of singularity which adheres to every particular content of consciousness. The apparently singular fact becomes known, understood, and conceptually grasped only in so far as it is "subsumed" under a general idea, recognized as a "case" of a law or as a member of a manifold or a series. In this sense every genuine judgment is synthetic; for what it intends and strives for is just this synthesis of parts into a whole, this weaving of particulars into a system. [14]

Let us then consider the possibility that the nuptial relation is the synthesis that underlies reason. Where modern philosophy (i.e., philosophy after Descartes) leaves mysterious the question of how we come to abstract universals of category and relation from concrete particulars of sense, classical metaphysics integrates these as aspects of one being that we can behold by taking them into our own being. We can do this because our being is nuptial; its spiritual form is the particulars of man and woman in the one universal God. Thus it is in our spirit to be able to discern both the particular and the universal in things.

Cassirer asks: "How can we know a thing as an instance of a class or kind?" How can we recognize case and category and hold their relation in mind? We can do this because we are in spirit both a *case* (a being unto ourselves, distinct from others) and a *category* (a oneness of male and female being in God). [15] By means of our own integration of case and category we can behold other integrations of case and category. We know other beings—birds, bees, bananas, boots, balls, bowties, boats—on the model of our own. [16] Understanding begins in the spirit of the nuptial relation. [17]

Although not spoken of in these terms by Aquinas, this nuptial image of reason is implicit in his language. He depicts reason as a meeting and merging of an outside-in movement of sensation in which a beholder receives the beheld and an inside-out movement of intellect in which a beholder acknowledges the beheld. The first registers the fact of *existence* which is always individual and singular—in Gilson's translation of Aquinas, "what the sense faculty knows materially and concretely, it knows directly as singular—the likeness which is in the senses is abstracted from the thing as from a knowable object, and therefore the thing itself is directly known through that likeness." [18] The second recognizes the fact of *essence*, what is abstractly intelligible, which is always universal—in Gilson's translation of Aquinas, "the universal is grasped while things are being understood, the singular while they are being sensed." [19] What is this integration of outside-in sensa tion and inside-out intellect, this all-at-once embrace of the particular and the universal, but a meeting and merging of the human female and male in spirit?

For St. Thomas the first act of knowing, what he called "sense," is an act of "adequation" by which we conform to the being of what we seek to know. It is literally a communication of being, to the knower from the known. This act, as we have seen, is the essentially feminine one of beholding (of holding in being) or "conformance" by which the knower takes the form of what is known. Aquinas scholar Jacques Maritain describes this act as "connatural," noting that it "is not clear like that obtained through concepts and conceptual judgments. It is obscure, unsystematic, vital knowledge, by means of instinct or sympathy, and in which the intellect, in order to make its judgments, consults the inner leanings of the subject."[20] It is a direct unmediated gleaning, perhaps not unlike that which the philosopher Charles Pierce called "abduction" and distinguished from induction and deduction.[21] The second act of knowing, for St. Thomas is that of the intellect or reason which discerns in the form thus beheld its abstract commonality with other forms to thereby give it a label or name. This act, as we have seen, is the essentially masculine one of finding the universal in the particular and projecting it as an idea.

Let us then entertain the "nuptial hypothesis" that the nuptial relation is the formal cause of human reason; that its synthesis of male and female in the image of God is the structure in and through which rational syntheses take place. This is to behold reason as nuptial being; to behold mind as a polarity of male and female that sparks the awareness of the conscious mind. And this is to understand Revelation as the key to self-understanding; we enjoy God's gift of mind as we fulfill His image as male and female in one flesh.

Efficient Cause of Reason

We have identified the nuptial relation as the material and formal cause of reason. How finally is it the efficient cause of reason? By what acts does it bring reason into being?

It is no banality to say, as we did in Chapter 1, that we are children of God, for the acts of reason by which we know His creation are natural to children and clearly to observe in them. We come into being by acts of reason that are three in type, nested in relation, and nuptial in form. These acts are at once the most human and most Godlike things about us.

The first and most basic act of our reason is *love*. This the child knows intuitively and without instruction as a bodily separateness overcome by the nurturing of his/her mother or caretaker. Love reaches across division to unity and reaches within unity to division. It marries female receptivity to other with male assertion of otherness. Love is explicit in the sexual relation where the woman opens to receive what the man musters to give. In its one flesh we are aware of love's truth and good that transcends the body (which is, again, why we can't shake the idea that sex is about more than pleasure). And love is implicit in mind and language. When we form an idea or give a name we likewise marry female receptivity to what is before us with male assertion of an idea or name. Love is rational because it is nuptial; because it unites male and female in the image of God.

Love takes shape in a second and related nuptial act of *play*. This the child knows, again intuitively and without instruction, as imagination; as a revel of fantasy within the bounds of reality. Play reaches across what can be (possibility) to what is (actuality) and reaches within what is to what can be. It marries female openness to possibility with male assertion of actuality. It is reason and will at the frontier of invention. It is love's leading edge which carves out new divisions and new unities of being. And it appears in human inventions of every kind—of new category and name in language, of winner and loser in games, of theatrical personae in stage plays, of melody and rhythm in music, of plot and story line in novels or film, and most generally of individual personality and group identity. Language is play as it marries a signifier, which is invented, to a signified, which is real. And games are play as they marry the statuses of "winner" and "loser," which are invented, to contestants, which are real. In language and game alike—and we could multiply examples *ad libitum*—play is the occasion of invention. In saying this about play we join anthropologist and linguist Johan Huizinga in supposing all things human—persons, societies, institutions, and cultures—are formed in play.[22]

And at last, whereas the nuptial act of love takes shape in the nuptial act of play, the latter comes to point in a final nuptial act of *fulfillment*. This the child knows, again intuitively and without instruction, as the finality of truth. Fulfillment reaches across the diversity of what is (actuality) to the unity of what must be (truth) and reaches within what must be to what is. It marries female care for actualities with male insistence upon the actuality that is true and before all others. Fulfillment is reason at the frontier of truth. It is play's leading edge (which again is love's leading edge) which carves out the true being of God. It is the spirit of man realized in the nuptial image and likeness of God which may be manifest in the body in sexual congress or in the mind in true ideas.[23] In Aristotle's terminology, fulfillment is the "final cause" by which we reach to God. Fulfillment is our nuptial longing without end, as we who are finite and mortal can never comprehend God Who is infinite and eternal. Our acts of fulfillment remind us that we can never know the fullness of truth. For us there is always more truth, more being, more God.

Thus we know God's being in nuptial acts of reason that are native to children and that are nested like Russian dolls. Before and encompassing all is God, who is Being itself. In God is love—the ground of reason in male division and female unity. In love is play—the leading edge of reason where male invention meets female reality. And in play is fulfillment—the final fruit of reason where female openness to actuality meets male insistence on truth. We become human—literally, come into our human being—as our love plays to the fulfillment of Truth. The nesting of our acts of reason is important because it means that reason does not necessarily or even usually lead to God. Not every act of love takes the shape of play and not every act of play is fulfilled in truth. There is solipsistic love closed-in on itself that invents nothing. And there is idle play that invents actualities that are not true. Thus while we are certainly made for God, it is only by a narrow gate that we can enter His kingdom.

Of course our human acts of reason—of love, play, and fulfillment—are but an infinitesimal part of God's Creation. Where His supreme intelligence has all things in mind and brings all things into being (including the great regularities of gravity, cosmic evolution, geology, ocean tides, plant and animal life, as well as the great particularities of our human persons), our vastly inferior intelligence has vastly more modest things in mind which it discerns and enacts (for examples we can write a poem, build a house, drive a car, or make a friend). And where His powers are infinite, our powers—however impressive they may be to us—are far more limited. Where He can create things from nothing—*creatio ex nihilo*—we can do no more than discern and name these things or else put them to use in sometimes novel ways. And while we call this last "creativity," it is nothing like the true creativity of God who is source and sustainer of all being. We are indeed as children to God.

It is well to emphasize, again, that we would have no reason and no human being if we were not the spiritual image of God. The nuptial relation is the material, formal, efficient, and final cause of reason and therefore of our being. This is to emphasize because it can hardly be understood today. Modern philosophy, observes philosopher Edward Feser, has abandoned the material, formal, efficient, and final causes of Aristotle's metaphysics and has visited upon itself thereby the catastrophes of mind-body dualism, nihilistic skepticism, logical positivism, and moral relativism.[24] And having done so, it cannot imagine that reason and mind have the nuptial bond as their substance, form, cause, and end. Feser supposes this crazy self-sabotage is motivated by eagerness to be rid of God and especially of His inconvenient moral dictates. We can add that perhaps there is eagerness as well to specifically deny the sanctity of the bond between man and woman. Certainly it is not easy in polite company today to affirm that we come into being—become human—only as we fulfill the true relation of man and woman in God.

CREATIVE REALISM

The sure sign that our reason—our conscious awareness in every form—is a gift from God is that by it we can know the truth. By our reason we discover being—not the "being" we invent for ourselves and demean by quotation marks, but real being. This is the being that every child knows but many or most modern philosophers have forgotten—the real world.

That our reason is metaphysical should not be surprising—for an idea is certainly not a physical object—but to me it is an abiding wonder that it is Divine. When I was young, I saw in reason only a human power of invention and idealization. I did not see that what we know must already have an essence and existence—a being— which is not our creation but is God's creation. I did not see that to reason is to discern—more or less sensitively and more or less truly—God's being in things. To look back on it now I see that this lesson—that we do not create things by reason but that God creates things for us to discern—was lost on me because I was a modern man who, after Descartes, believed that ideas (mind) exist apart from things (body), and who, after his own ego, sought to create himself with ideas such as 'family provider,' 'wise and loving father,' 'academic genius,' 'hero to students,' 'champion athlete,' 'extraordinary lover' etc… Only lately have I come to see why my efforts at world and self-invention could only fail. Only lately have I come to see that I cannot create either because God creates both. This, again, is what it means to be a child of God; and this, again, is what it means to be a spirit in beloved relation to the infinite, eternal, and perfect Supreme Being who is beyond every name or category. Because God speaks the world and my being, these are unspeakable to me.

Between these opposed conceptions—between ideal and real, physical and metaphysical, and godless and God-full—goes the moral struggle of our reason and therefore of our being in the world. Our good is to take part in God's ongoing creation by free acts of reason that are at once personal (we perform them in person) and communal (we perform then in league with others). This is our personal and communal good of creative realism; of discerning and giving name to the real being of God who is Being itself. This is the awe, wonder, and beauty of our reason; that it is at once "involved-in" and "about" the being of the one, true, real God who created us in His image to take part in the joy of His ongoing Creation.

NOTES

1. C.S. Lewis, "*De Futilitate*," Christian Reflections (Walter Hooper, ed.) (Grand Rapids, MI: William B. Eerdmans, 1995, p. 65).

2. Edward Feser, *Aquinas* (Oxford, England: Oneworld, 2009).

3. Martin Buber, *I and Thou* (trans. By Ronald G. Smith) (New York: Charles Scribner's Sons, 1958).

4. Owen Barfield, *Saving the Appearances, 2e* (Middletown, CT: Wesleyan University Press, 1988).

5. Etienne Gilson, *Methodical Realism* (trans. by Philip Trower) (San Francisco: Ignatius Press, 2011), p. 38.

6. For a more extensive description of how the forms of human society originate in and are sustained by the functional relating of male and female, see my book, Lloyd Sandelands, *Male and Female in Social Life* (New Brunswick, NJ: Transaction, 2001). In that book, however, I had not yet come to see that this relating depends for its integrity upon a unifying third term. In a word, I had not yet come to see that this relating rests in God.

7. The discussion in this section borrows from my *Man and Nature in God* (New Brunswick, NJ: Transaction, 2005), pp. 32-40.

8. The precursors of family appear in the primary order of social life described earlier. Among our mammalian ancestors the clamor of hierarchy-obsessed males to impress choosy females produced only brief impersonal assignations—flings with no strings. Females mated the highest-ranking males (in some species the alpha male almost exclusively) and, once pregnant, left the sexual stage to care for the young, sometimes in league with other females. Later, females of certain primate species (including precursors to modern baboons, chimpanzees, and humans), granted sexual favors also to males who consistently helped them with food and children—males that could be described as 'friends;' see Barbara Smuts, *Sex and Friendship in Baboons* (New York: Aldine de Gruyter, 1985). This inaugurated a sexual economy in which males were sexually rewarded not only for being dominant, but also for being reliably helpful. This development was crucial because it meant that a great many more males could gain access to females. In principle, if not in fact, every male could befriend a female and thereby gain mating chances that otherwise belonged to the dominant male.

9. So congenial is family to human existence that we might ask if it was a consequence of our ancestors' migration onto the savannah or a factor contributing to this migration. With family to stabilize relations between the sexes, females could cooperate in mutual support with minimal concern for who among them would capture the attention and resources of which males, while males could cooperate for mutual gain in group tasks with likewise minimal concern about which of them would mate which females. Family facilitates cooperation within and between sexes; see H.E. Fisher, *The Sex Contract: Evolution of Human Behavior* (New York: William Morrow, 1982).

10. The psychology of this functional unity is perhaps familiar. In the most robust men's or women's groups there is a hint of family, and likewise in the warmest and coziest domestic scene there is a brooding presence of single sex groups. One enters a men's or women's group in part to leave family behind and in part to prepare for a return. Men learn to compete fairly with other men so as to be attractive to women. Women learn to make wise choices and to care for young so as to be attractive to men. By the same token, one seeks a family life in part to leave the men's or women's group behind and in part to set the stage for a return. In the family, men and women learn how the other feels, thinks, and acts. However, while love of mate and love of children make man and woman whole, this comes at the risk of losing one's sexual identity, which must be reclaimed in the same sex group.

11. This actuality is unprecedented in animal life and it changes everything about human life. Where other animals *have* parts in the life of the species (think of castes of social insects or sexual divisions of labor in mammals), people *play* parts in the life of the species. For example, whereas a worker bee never worries its destiny and never thinks to throw off the chains that bind it to the hive, people worry all the time about who they are and about their duties to others. A man is no pigeon in a pecking order; he is a self- and socially-aware member of a group. Hierarchy for him is at once a physical fact and mental idea. Ranks in the hierarchy are "roles" played by more or less interchangeable group members.

12. Karl Stern, *The Flight from Woman* (New York: Farrar, Straus & Giroux, 1965), p. xx. See also my *Male and Female in Social Life* (New Brunswick, NJ: Transaction, 2001).

13. Ernst Cassirer, *Language and Myth* (New York: Dover, 1953), p. 36.

14. Ibid, p. 26.

15. Our grasp of this relation is perhaps facilitated by our uniquely human form of conjugal congress. In meeting face to face, male and female open their eyes upon the soul of the other.

16. This is perhaps the highest-level instance of what Susanne Langer, in *Mind: An Essay in Human Feeling* (Baltimore, MD: Johns Hopkins University, 1967), described as the organic basis of psychic life in the growth and development of acts. She believed that psychic life—sensations and feelings—began in the interplay of organisms with their environments: "The importance of the periphery holds for all creatures, no matter what their degree of complexity, size or behavioral freedom; and especially in free-living animals, which may enter new environments, the structural articulation of the surface membranes plays a leading part in the evolution of their organization" p. 419. Furthermore, "The great evolutionary importance of this constant and inveterate activity of the peripheral surface in animals is that it probably engenders the first acts of such intensity that they enter a psychical phase, a moment of intra-organic appearance as sensation" p. 424. What is unique and unprecedented in our human case is that as man and woman we take part in a transcendental unity of nuptial relation through which we come to a new categorical and linguistic awareness. This new awareness is an absolute, indeed cataclysmic, break in the story of evolution. In our kind uniquely, organic sensations and feelings taking place at the periphery of the body rise to the level of meaning. In our kind uniquely, dyadic biology engenders triadic mind.

17. One might ask, as did my late friend and colleague Michael Cohen, how the nuptial relation could be the basis of categorical understanding if that understanding first appears in children who cannot know of the nuptial relationship until they are adults. Indeed, might the causation be the other way around, that categorical understanding in children prepares the way for the nuptial relation in adults? The metaphysical answer, I believe, is that the nuptial form is written into our very creation by God as male and female in one flesh. Thus the nuptial form is not acquired by experience but is available to our understanding from the beginning of life. While a bodily realization of this form must await physical maturation, its spiritual realization need not be so delayed.

18. Etienne Gilson, *Methodical Realism*, p. 57.

19. Ibid, p. 57.

20. Jacques Maritain, *Natural Law* (South Bend, IN: St. Augustine's Press, 2001), pp. 34-35.

21. Arthur W. Burks, "Pierce's evolutionary pragmatic idealism," *Synthese, 106(3),* 1996, pp. 323-372.

22. Johan Huizinga, *Homo Ludens* (Boston: Beacon Press, 1950).

23. Here, in the truth of God, the ways of sex and reason converge. Given the mess that so many of us make of our lives, one wonders which way be the surer to God!

24. Edward Feser, *The Last Superstition* (South Bend, IN: St. Augustine's Press, 2008).

Chapter Three

To Be or Not to Be

Many of us today fancy ourselves "self-made." With the philosopher Descartes we imagine that we need only think to be: "I think, therefore I am." We don't see how we are "unmade" by this idea; how by accepting it we take part in a lie, spiritual error, and offense against the One who is the source of all being.

The truth is that we cannot think our way into being. While we can think *about* our self—we do all the time—we cannot think *up* our self. We cannot conjure or even understand our self because we cannot stand apart from our self to do the conjuring or understanding. As Walker Percy points out:

> The fateful flaw of human semiotics is this: that of all the objects in the entire Cosmos which the sign-user can apprehend through the conjoining of signifier and signified (word uttered and thing beheld), there is one which forever escapes his comprehension—and that is the sign-user himself. Semiotically, the self is literally unspeakable to itself … The semiotic history of this creature thereafter could be written in terms of the successive attempts, both heroic and absurd, of the signifying creature to escape its nakedness and to find a permanent semiotic habiliment for itself. [1]

Few today have lamented our failures of self-conjuring as roundly as writer David Foster Wallace, who saw that our troubles begin with the absurd idea that we are the world:

> A huge percentage of the stuff that I tend to be automatically certain of is, it turns out, totally wrong and deluded. Here's one example of the utter wrongness of something I tend to be automatically sure of: Everything in my own immediate experience supports my deep belief that I am the absolute center of the universe, the realest, most vivid and important person in existence. We

rarely talk about this sort of natural, basic self-centeredness, because it's so
socially repulsive, but it's pretty much the same for all of us, deep down.[2]

When our basic self-centeredness, with its implacable desire to think well
of self, meets the impossibility of secure self-knowledge, the result is an
insatiable rush for self-esteem. We want to be great, but we see ourselves
small. We want to be loved, but we know we merit only disgust and disap-
proval. We want to be beautiful, but beauty's bloom quickly fades. We want
the truth about ourselves, but we despise any who would share it with us.
And we want every consoling pleasure, but find that all lose their savor.

How pathetic can we be? Though blessed to be in the world, we are
unhappy, and worse, ungrateful. And though surrounded by love of family,
friends, even complete strangers, we feel denied and deprived. Desperate for
being we grab for it in every direction—in our work, in others, in diversions
and amusements, and in easy pleasures and escapes. And when our chase for
being does not avail, we do crazy neurotic things that only enlarge our want.
We seek for self in possessions or experiences. We gaze as Narcissus into
mirrors or Google searches or Facebook pages or into the eyes of adoring
others. And still we want. When our efforts to be fail, as they must, we grow
angry with the cruel world. And when our anger boils to a rage we turn
against ourselves in depression. Ours is a crisis of being in the world and,
today more than ever, we have the anxiety and depression to prove it.

For Wallace, our crisis of being is a crisis of what to worship. There is no
such thing as atheism, he says, because, whether we know it or admit it or
not, we always worship something:

> The only choice we get is *what* to worship. And an outstanding reason for
> choosing some sort of God or spiritual-type thing to worship or some infran-
> gible set of ethical principles—is that pretty much anything else you worship
> will eat you alive. If you worship money and things—if they are where you tap
> real meaning in life—then you will never have enough. Never feel you have
> enough. It's the truth. Worship your own body and beauty and sexual allure
> and you will always feel ugly, and when time and age start showing, you will
> die a million deaths before they finally plant you. On one level, we all know
> this stuff already—it's been codified as myths, proverbs, clichés, bromides,
> epigrams, parables: the skeleton of every great story. The trick is keeping the
> truth up-front in daily consciousness.[3]

Our unknowable and inconsolable being gives reason to Pope Benedict
XVI's warning that "a person's development is compromised if he claims to
be solely responsible for producing what he becomes."[4] "Being" is not for us
but only for God to create. We come into being only as we come into Him.

YOU CAN'T GET THERE FROM HERE

We struggle to be because that is what God asks of us. We are His beloved, the ones for whom He waits. He gives us the reason and grace we need to come to Him, but He leaves it to us to do so, to choose Him before all other things.

Being is a challenge for us because of how we think about it. We do not think about being as did Aristotle and Aquinas, who conceived of it metaphysically as an actuality of material, formal, efficient, and final potencies that can be rationally understood. To the contrary, we think about being as did Descartes and Bacon, who conceived of it scientifically as dyadic interactions of objects and events in space and time that can be empirically perceived. Ours today is the burden of scientism which rests on two delusions: one of objectivity (that the world consists only of matter in motion), the other of subjectivity (that the world is as we see it). We must overcome these delusions to become truly human.

The Delusion of Objectivity

It was with the Enlightenment and the scientific era it ushered that we first thought about the world in objective terms. That's when we decided that the world is matter and energy in space and time and that it is to know by the measure of its objects (e.g., size, weight, color, temperature, movement, etc…). That's when we made ourselves master of all things. The model for our takeover of the world has been natural science, so-called because by it we turn all things into "nature." As C.S. Lewis notes:

> We reduce things to mere Nature *in order that* we may 'conquer' them. We are always conquering Nature, *because* 'Nature' is the name for what we have, to some extent, conquered. The price of conquest is to treat a thing as mere Nature. Every conquest over Nature increases her domain. The stars do not become Nature till we can weigh and measure them: the soul does not become Nature till we can psychoanalyze her. [5]

Natural science is the idol of the age; and we are its cult. The danger in it—aside from its hubris which will one day humble us (if it has not already)—is that it leads us from open fields of real being into dark woods of our own making. We lose sight of the metaphysical truth that there are no "mere objects" in the cosmos. We forget that even the most inert matter or simplest creature—a block of ice or a single-celled organism—is *being*; is an actuality wrought from potencies by material, formal, efficient, and final causes. We suppose that because we *can* see such a thing simply as an object, and *can* relate such a thing to other things simply in dyads of cause and effect, that it *is* simply an object and that it *is* simply a cause or effect. But just because we *can* turn a robin's song, or a daffodil's perfume, or a summer sunset's festival into a story about objects in cause-effect relations, does not mean that we should. This, according to psychologist and linguist Owen Barfield, is the error of failing to "save the appearances;" the error of failing to bear in mind that what we see is not the real thing but is always an "appearance" of the real thing. And this is the error that romantic poet William Wordsworth had in mind when he observed that "we murder to dissect." Natural science, whatever its popularity and prestige, is no reason to deny or ignore the real being of things.

It is therefore metaphysical due diligence to not regard things as objects, but to appreciate them as beings. Our world is not only to see, but is even more to behold. This is true of everything, but of nothing more surely than human persons. Where we might excuse natural science for treating matter or simple creatures as objects—especially if the aim is to use them for practical purposes—we cannot excuse it for treating persons as objects—especially if the aim is to use them for practical purposes. To treat anything as an object is to commandeer its existence. It is to subordinate it to our self who, godlike, "creates" and "sustains" it in thought. Such arrogance may be hard to see or to get exercised about in the case of simple things whose being is banal or hard hold in mind, but it is unconscionable in the case of a human person whose being is like our own, fashioned in the image of God. Then we see our claim of objectivity for the delusion it is; then we see it as a theft from God who creates and sustains all being.

The metaphysical theft that marks the human sciences—which are as proud of their objectivity as any natural or physical science—is more subtle and for that reason more dangerous in our ordinary thinking about ourselves. As noted above, ours is a frantic and often neurotic search for identity. We cling to the "objective" registers of modern life—to its gradations of wealth, role, rank, and status. In this we are surely the children of a scientific age; we see our self and others as things to be sized and weighed. And so we seek our self in outer signs; in the eyes and reactions of others (as if they know us better than we do) and in the many and varied mirrored surfaces that reflect us back to ourselves. We see our self as do the sociologists and philosophers. Sociologist Charles Cooley wrote of our "looking glass self;" sociologists Peter Berger and Thomas Luckmann of our "social construction of reality"; philosopher George William Friedrich Hegel of our "objectification of the subject;" and lately, philosopher Roger Scruton of our "imprinting" of self on what we are not.[6] Writes Scruton: "Through the life of civil society, through religion, art and institutions, I shape myself as an other in the eyes of others, and so gain consciousness of myself as a subject who acts freely in the a world that I share."[7] In this idea of how we come to be, we forget what it is to be. We reduce our being to a mere object in the minds of others; we are a "self" in a world of selves, a social construct. And thinking this way, we forget the first of all facts, that we are not an identity but a being in the image of God. We forget that while our identity may be to discern among the reactions, reflections, and good impressions of others—reactions, reflections, and impressions that are of one object upon another—our being is something else again and is to find only in the One who creates and sustains all being.

What is more and worse, we regard ourselves and others as objects so that we can to put them to use. When a military commander marshals soldiers for battle, he thinks of them not specifically as persons like himself, but generally as "personnel" or even more impersonally as "forces." It is easier to put personnel or forces to strategic objectives, especially if there is a chance they may be killed. And when a business executive deploys workers in trade, he thinks of them not specifically as persons like himself, but generally as "labor" or again even more impersonally as "human resources." But we hardly need such clichés to make the point. We have arranged nearly a billion people into networks such as Facebook and LinkedIn so that we can call on them when we want. We contract with people in the marketplace to meet our needs and desires. We think of others and ourselves, not as beings, but as commodities.

The moral hazard in regarding persons as objects is clearest in pornography, rape, and genocide. These are 'crimes against humanity' because they negate the reason and freedom that define human persons. Theirs is a degrading impersonality. Pornography abandons the tenderness of love—in it there is little kissing or even face-to-face contact; and in it what is "private" is exposed for public consumption. The pornographer, his actors, and audience conspire to diminish the person to a mere body, to an object without being. Rape plies its inhumanity in a more heinous way; the rapist forces upon his victim not only his unwanted body but the catastrophic idea that she or he (the victim) is nothing more than a body without being. And genocide takes inhumanity to its terrible end. By objectifying an entire people (a race, ethnicity, or family), it takes the final downhill step to treat them as refuse to discard or as vermin to exterminate. While we are quick to condemn genocide as a vicious inhumanity and to punish it as a capital offense, and quick too to regard rape in the same way even if we don't punish it the same way, we are not only less condemning but even tolerant and in some quarters approving of pornography. Do we think that it does not offend human being? That it does not have victims?

It is not an insignificant detail that the humiliations of pornography, rape, and genocide deny human being by denying the image of God in the nuptial union of male and female. This is the purpose of pornography, the theft of rape, and the horror of genocide (which often includes rape and always destroys marriages and families). But terrible as these crimes are, their like are to find everywhere. There is a parallel if more innocent-seeming corruption of the nuptial relation and a parallel if smaller-written dissipation of humanity to find on the university campus today.[8] The objectifying tendency that has turned sex on campus from a divine nuptial relation between a man and a woman to a dissolute "hook-up" between variously gendered strangers or "friends with benefits," is the same tendency that has turned the rational mind on campus from the playful realism of truth-seeking to the dismal materialism of natural science. The moral crisis born of objectivity—both in its extreme crimes against humanity and in its milder infractions of sexual license and close-mindedness in the university—is its denial of our human being which is denial of our God.

The Delusion of Subjectivity

As our final cause and greatest good, reason gives substance, form, efficacy and purpose to all of our other goods, which are "goods" in the measure that they lead to or support our greatest good. Reason is good because it is awareness of God. The nuptial union of male and female is good because it engenders and supports reason. Family is good because it justifies and sustains the nuptial union. A secure job that pays a living family wage and that engages the heart and mind is good because it enables the worker to grow and develop as a person who can enter into nuptial union and start a family. And so it goes for every good—a supportive circle of friends, a safe and secure physical environment, a community that works for the common good, a civil society under the rule of law, a political process in which everyone can participate, a world committed to peace between nations, and so on—each is good as it supports the greatest good of reason which is being in God.

Thus it is for us to live in and according to God by putting Him first in our lives and by seeking those other goods that support our being in Him. This is the challenge we routinely fail because of our second delusion of subjectivity. As noted above, we are authorized and encouraged by our modern scientific outlook to distinguish between the world as it is objectively given and ourselves as we subjectively experience it. This bifurcation is trouble enough when it comes to declaring truths (for this we must rely on agreements between subjects), but it is especially vexing when it comes to deciding goods. Thanks in no small part to the skeptical philosophy of David Hume we today dismiss questions of the good as unscientific. Science, we say, is about what *is,* not about what *ought* to be.[9] What ought to be, says Hume, is not to discern in the nature of things, but is to ascribe to things as a sentiment. Science then can teach nothing of the good. What is "good" is subjective and personal—it is not "one-size-fits-all" but is for each to decide. Contemporary philosopher Alasdair MacIntyre calls this outlook "emotivism;" it is the idea that "all evaluative judgments and more specifically all moral judgments are nothing but expressions of preference, expressions of attitude or feeling, insofar as they are moral or evaluative in character."[10] As MacIntyre notes, this doctrine is not a positive claim about what is truly good or truly moral, but is a negative claim that there can be no true good or true morality.

Much like the claim of objectivity, with which it coexists in the modern mind, the claim of subjectivity is motivated. It casts aside the question of being—and thereby the questions of truth, beauty, and good—for the sake of a simple rule for life: to live for oneself by one's lights according to one's desires. And what a congenial rule it is for an age that wants no part of an absolute moral code, least of all one that condemns its polymorphous sexual desires. Subjectivity is the ideal of a liberated life celebrated in the 18th century by Jean Jacques Rousseau, in the 19th century by Sigmund Freud, and in the 20th century by the philosopher John Rawls, all of whom share the idea that the moral order is not absolute and not given by God, but is a culturally-specific social consciousness that, in addition to being arbitrary, may be false and oppressive to individuals. [11] The good of human being, on this account, is a social fiction, as would be any "god" alleged to create this being.

Subjectivity is the evil of denying the truth and good of God. As Aquinas noted, the subject of evil is the good. Evil is not its own malevolent force, not one half of a Manichean contest, but is the absence or privation of the good. And the privation of subjectivity is our being in the image and likeness of God. In it we turn from God in two ways. One is by denying the authority of His truth and good. This is the poison fruit of atheism which supposes, with the moral philosopher John Rawls, that reason by itself—i.e., reason uninformed by faith—is enough to establish the bounds of good and evil. For his part, Rawls defines the good as the allocation of resources people will choose if placed under a "veil of ignorance" in which they cannot know their relative endowments or merits. [12] Then, he says, people will distribute resources equally unless an unequal distribution is to the advantage of the least favored. The problem with this morality is that while its end result may be clear (although this is debatable), its means is not. There is no telling what a person must do, only that whatever he does it must not come at the expense of others and particularly at the expense of the least favored. The other way we turn from God is by putting some other good before Him. In this second way we might at least have a good intention—we might intend a good while mistaking its priority. But hell's road is paved with good intentions.

Being in the Balance

And so we struggle to be. Ours is a struggle against the world. It is a struggle particularly against concupiscence; of our immortal spirit against a balky wayward mortal body. But it is a struggle also against society; again of our immortal spirit against cultural mores and folkways that distract or divert it from God. The Christian message is that there is a battle between spirit and world to fight and win. "There is no true Christianity," wrote Etienne Gilson, "without contempt for the world."[13] This contempt, he argued, is not a hatred of being; rather it is a hatred of non-being—such as the non-being of a person lost to self-love, pleasure-seeking, or empty amusement, or the non-being of a community lost to worldly striving, wealth, celebrity or tribal animosities. And while our struggle for being ends with our mortal lives, the stakes couldn't be higher because our bodily death is an eternal sentence to spiritual damnation or spiritual beatitude.

Our struggle to be is personal; the unique story of a uniquely given being. But while unique in particulars, it is also a story of universal human being. Every person comes to be as a conversion—from the non-being of sin to the being of God—and as an amazing grace—from being lost to being found. This is why we can see ourselves in any person's becoming, such as that famously told by St. Augustine in his *Confessions*. His was the struggle we all know; "I am," he wrote, "fitted for life here where I do not want to be, I want to live there [in Heaven, with God] but am unfit for it, and on both counts I am miserable."[14] Before his conversion to God, Augustine lived in the world of personal subjectivity; the world of objects for his taking; the world of personal pleasures (often carnal it seems); the world of no purpose or meaning greater than his self. This was the residence that he abandoned only reluctantly, famously asking God to free him from his sins, particularly his fleshly wants, "but not yet." This was the residence that he came to see as certainly disappointing and self-destructive, but only after his faith matured to the point when he could gather-up his will and turn himself over to God. When that happened, wrote Augustine:

> For me, good things were no longer outside, no longer quested for by fleshly eyes in this world's sunlight. Those who want to find their joy in externals all too easily grow empty themselves. They pour themselves out on things which, being seen, are but transient, and lick even the images of these things with the famished imaginations. If only they would weary of their starvation and ask, *Who will show us the good things?* [15]

The "who" for the saint was Jesus Christ. And the "good things" for the saint were the truth, good, and beauty of God. He saw "truth" as Revelation elaborated and extended by reason. He saw "good" as putting God's will first and before his own. And he saw "beauty" as the pleasures of God's Creations. Being, he saw, is to seek in those human perfections in which we are an image of God; of His unity, immutability, truth, goodness, beauty, eternity, and holiness. In His image we appear anew, not as a material and sensate being that will pass away, but as a spiritual being eternal as He is eternal.

After his conversion St. Augustine saw that his hope of salvation was in the Lord God and in the Lord God alone. Again the Saint, here addressing our Lord:

In truth you are Being itself, unchangeable, and in you is found the rest that is mindful no more of its labors, for there is no one else beside you, nor need our rest concern itself with striving for a host of other things that are not what you are; rather it is you, *you Lord, who through hope establish me in unity.*[16]

Our hope must be to join that of the saint. With Bishop Bossuet, we can hope to understand that "Wisdom lies in knowing God and knowing oneself" and that "from knowledge of self we rise to knowledge of God."[17] And with theologian Etienne Gilson, we can hope to see that insatiability of our world-ly desires means that we are attracted by an infinite good and that our disgust with ourselves is the reverse of our thirst for Him.[18] And so with these wise souls we must acknowledge what our life proves beyond all doubt; that the fateful choice to be is our own. Either we must be content with goods that cannot content us or we must renounce our worldly desires so as not to wear ourselves out trying to "appease a hunger reborn with every sop that is flung to it."[19]

If we cannot answer the question of being: "Who am I?" it is for the simple reason that only God knows. Indeed, it better for us not to try because any answer we come to on our own will certainly be mistaken and mislead-ing (literally *mis-leading*, as it will lead us not to God but away from God). The best we can do—the thing we must do—is to let our self be small so that He may be large in us. We must empty our self that He may fill us up; we must die to our self that we be reborn in Him. To our contemporary scientific mind, identity, self, and ego are the objects that we create and put to the use of our subject. Better that we not seek a self but seek Him in Whom we come to be. Let us close this section by recalling its leading idea that when it comes to being "you can't get there from here;" where "here" is our human world— our world uninformed by God, our evil-ridden world of human ends put before God, our world of casual sex without nuptial meaning; our world of degraded reason unmoored from being and pre-occupied with every want— and where "there" is being in God. We have made a mess of the world because we have made a mess of our being by thinking with the delusions of the modern world, thinking we can be as gods by making the world for ourselves. The proof that we cannot is in the pudding.

THE (VERY BEARABLE) LIGHTNESS OF BEING

Given that we are unable to claim it for ourselves, it is ironic if not positively comic that our being is not actually a problem. In the word and example of Jesus Christ we have the living lesson that our being is sure to find, not in the here and now of this our human world, but in the everywhere and forever of the Kingdom of the Father. This is the lesson guaranteed by the passion of Christ which gave final victory to joy over grief, to life over death, to being over non-being. In Christ, our trials and tribulations fall away; in Christ, our burden is light and our yoke is easy. How perverse then that so many today put death before life in the bleak existentialism of a Sartre or Camus, the dark nihilism of a Nietzsche, the angry atheism of a Dawkins or Hitchens, the maddening materialism of Madison Avenue, or the empty celebrity of Hollywood. It is simply not our nature to be bleak, cynical, angry, mad, or empty. "Man," writes Chesterton, "is more himself, man is more manlike, when joy is the fundamental thing in him, and grief the superficial."[20] Men suffer for being unable to see their estate truly, to see how their lives "run over" with the love of God that is being itself.

Ways of Being

As we are not *of* the world, but of the One who creates and sustains the world, we come into being as we come into God. But what does this mean? What is it to be in God? Here again, as always, we have the word of Jesus Christ to go on. In his *Sermon on the Mount* he teaches us exactly what the blessedness of beatitude—being in God—means. As set forth in the Gospel of Matthew 5, it consists of eight distinct beatitudes, eight different things we should want if we want to be in God and to be thereby humanly perfected.

And seeing the multitudes, He went up on a mountain, and when He was seated His disciples came to Him. [2] *Then He opened His mouth and taught them, saying:*
[3] *Blessed are the poor in spirit,*
For theirs is the kingdom of heaven.
[4] *Blessed are those who mourn,*
For they shall be comforted.
[5] *Blessed are the meek,*
For they shall inherit the earth.
[6] *Blessed are those who hunger and thirst for righteousness,*
For they shall be filled.
[7] *Blessed are the merciful,*
For they shall obtain mercy.
[8] *Blessed are the pure in heart,*
For they shall see God.
[9] *Blessed are the peacemakers,*
For they shall be called sons of God.
[10] *Blessed are those who are persecuted for righteousness' sake,*
For theirs is the kingdom of heaven.
[11] *Blessed are you when they revile and persecute you, and say all kinds of evil against you falsely for My sake.*
[12] *Rejoice and be exceedingly glad, for great is your reward in heaven, for so they persecuted the prophets who were before you.*

These eight beatitudes, as philosopher Peter Kreeft points out, are not the sorts of things we usually think of as desirable; indeed they are generally the opposite of what we usually think of as desirable.[21] First, where we think it is blessed to have wealth, Christ insists to the contrary that we are blessed to be able to live without it. "The poor in spirit," notes Kreeft, "are not the weak-spirited; they are exactly the opposite. They are strong enough to be detached from riches, that is, from the whole world. They are those who are strong enough not to be enslaved to their desires for the things of this world."[22] Second, where we think of loss as an agony, Christ instructs to the contrary that we are blessed to mourn. Mourning expresses our inner discontent, our suffering in the knowledge that we cannot have all that we want. "Christ came not to free us from suffering," which we cannot escape, "but to transform its meaning, to make it salvic. He came to save us from sin, and he did so precisely by embracing the suffering and death that are the result of sin."[23] Third, where we thirst for honor, fame and glory, and where we applaud triumph and conquest, Christ turns the table to say that we are blessed to be meek. "The meek," says Kreeft, "are those who do not harm, who do not see life as competitive, because they understand the two premises from which this conclusion logically follows: First, that the best things in life are spiritual things, not material things … and second, … that spiritual things are not competitive. That they multiply when shared, while material things are divided when shared."[24] Fourth, where we today think our greatest good is self-esteem and self-satisfaction, Christ judges us blessed to hunger and thirst for righteousness, to be dissatisfied with ourselves, and particularly dissatisfied with our sins and our failures of sanctity. Christ does not suppose that this hunger and thirst for righteousness is satisfied only in the next life, but that it is satisfied even in this one. As Kreeft notes, "Already in this life, the saints have a peace and a joy that the world cannot give. They are at the same time dissatisfied and satisfied, like Romeo with Juliet, like you listening to a great symphony, or watching a great storm at sea."[25] Fifth, where we want to be treated fairly, to have justice for ourselves, to have our rights observed and honored, Christ says that we are blessed to be merciful, to give rather than to receive, and especially to give without expecting to receive. After all, and as we well know, only by divine mercy can we be forgiven our sins and united with God, and so only by our mercy to one another can we together attain to the divine nature. Sixth, where we have little interest in resisting or confining in any way our desires, especially those for sex which bring an immediate thrill of delight, Christ says that we are blessed to be pure of heart, to enjoy our desires in their natural, proper, God-given measure. The harm in unbridled desire, as noted by many, including the great Doctors of the Church, St. Augustine, St. Thomas, and St. John of the Cross, is that it blinds the reason that makes us human. Enflamed by intemperate desire, we lose perspective and find it hard to act intelligently for our true good. Lust, as every adolescent boy knows, trumps reason.[26] Seventh, where we long for peace, for an end to all conflict and war, Christ corrects us to point out that we are blessed to be peace-makers, to be those who bring His peace, the peace of God. Peacemaking is not pacifism, but a spiritual war against conflict and war. "Happiness," adds Kreeft, "does not consist in pacifism; happiness consists in peace, and peace can be obtained only by waging and winning a war to make peace." Eighth and finally, where the last thing we want is to be disrespected, rejected, and unloved by others, Christ says that we are blessed to be persecuted for righteousness' sake. How can it be a blessing to be hated? As Kreeft points out, "the reward that makes persecution blessed is the same as the one that makes poverty blessed: the kingdom of Heaven. Persecution has the same blessing as poverty because persecution is a form of poverty, poverty not of money, but of love, that is, of being loved. Both money and love are blessed only when they are given: *It is more blessed to give than to receive.*"[27]

In the eight Beatitudes we come into being, into the one and only being that is God. In whatever measure we attain it, being is always a reach upward from our fallen condition of sin to a merciful Father. This is no doleful or regretful project, but its merry and liberating opposite. Surprising to say, God's love for us is *fun.* In reading the New Testament gospels, Chesterton found in Christ an enigmatic restraint, a certain shyness and "holding back" from his apostles and disciples. Chesterton wondered, what was too great for God to show man when as Christ He walked on earth? Chesterton fancied that it was mirth.[28] God, it seems, has created the world so that He can laugh with us in the fun of it all. This is something like the idea Bishop Fulton Sheen had in mind when he wrote of our need for a "sense of Divine Humor;" a need he thought that is answered especially in the story of Christmas:

> Man loses his sense of humor through sin. He begins to take money seriously, flesh seriously, business seriously, food seriously. These have no other purpose than just to satisfy him. Now Christmas Day was the restoration of humor, and those who displayed it most were the shepherds and the wise men. They came to this little Babe and "saw through Him"—God Himself. His Flesh was the Sacrament of His Divinity. When the Babe grew, He taught parables in or with a sense of Divine Humor. Salt and camels, sheep and goats, patches on old clothing, wine in old bottles, businessmen, traders, were not to be taken seriously. All were telltale of something else. Christmas then is a romance and a joy only to those who have a sense of humor, whose vision is not opaque when they look at a Babe, but can see through Him all the problems of life answered in the vision of God Who appeared as a Man. They who pass through this life with that sense of humor, which is faith, will one day be rewarded by the one thing that will make heaven Heaven—His Smile.[29]

To Be What We Are

As we have seen, it is our fate today to live between worlds—between the un-metaphysical and godless world of science and the metaphysical and God-full world of reason informed by faith. Our modern life is a test to reach to the second even while our feet of clay are planted in the first. It is a test we cannot afford to fail because we cannot flourish in or even survive in a world without God. As the philosopher Edward Feser points out:

> …without keeping in mind that our ultimate destiny is an eternal one and that knowing God is our natural end or purpose (even if it is left to us, as beings with free will, to decide whether to pursue and realize that end), our under-standing of our lives in the here and now, including our understanding of morality, becomes massively distorted. This life, in both its good and bad aspects, takes on an exaggerated importance. Worldly pleasures and projects become overvalued. Difficult moral obligations, which seem bearable in light of the prospect of an eternal reward, come to seem impossible to live up to when our horizons are this-worldly. Harms and injustices suffered in this life, patiently endured when one sees beyond it to the next life, suddenly become unendurable.[30]

Ours is the struggle to put God before all things and to see all things in true perspective. It is a struggle because modern life conspires against us. Life today is a contemptible chaos of deformity and diversion. It beckons us with outer temptations when our inner being is to find in God who wishes to recognize himself in us. Life today is "evil" insofar as it deprives us of the being of God. As we will see in the next chapter, our business world particularly is today contemptible as it leads away from God. But as we will see also, our business world is today laudable as it brings us to God.

The paradox of our being is that while we cannot bring it about but must rely on the grace of God who creates all being, the choice to be is nevertheless ours to make. By reason and will we can choose life in God or death in sin. The key for us is Christ who is our God-given image of "being"—our Word and Way. We come to be as we imitate him; as we come into God the Father as he came into God the Father, through reason and will. We are fulfilled as Christ was and is eternally fulfilled, through that love and play that leads to the Father.

NOTES

1. Walker Percy, *Lost in the Cosmos* (New York: Farrar, Straus & Giroux, 1983), pp. 106, 108.

2. David Foster Wallace, *This is Water*, Commencement Speech to Kenyon College, 2005, Gambier, OH; http://www.youtube.com/watch?v=M5THXa_H_N8.

3. *Ibid.*

4. Pope Benedict XVI, *Caritas in Veritate*, www.vatican.va/holy_father/benedict_xvi/encyclicals, #68.

5. C.S. Lewis, *The Abolition of Man* (San Francisco: Harper, 2001), p. 71.

6. Charles Horton Cooley, *Human Nature and the Social Order* (New Brunswick, NJ: Transaction, 1983); Peter L. Berger and Thomas Luckmann, *The Social Construction of Reality* (Garden City, NY: Anchor Books, 1966); George William Friedrich Hegel, *The Phenomenology of Spirit*, tr. A. Miller (Oxford: Clarendon Press, 1977, pp. 111-118); Roger, Scruton, *The Face of God* (London: Continuum, 2012, p. 64).

7. Scruton, *The Face of God*, p. 64.

8. Lloyd Sandelands, *The Nuptial Mind* (Lanham, MD: University Press of America, 2012); Allan Bloom, *The Closing of the American Mind* (New York: Simon and Schuster, 1988).

9. This familiar saying, however, is misleading. While science is not about what *ought* to be, it is also not about what *is*. The latter is the subject of metaphysics, the subject upon which science depends for its being.

10. Alasdair MacIntyre, *After Virtue, 2e* (Notre Dame, IN: Notre Dame University Press, 1984), p. 11-12.

11. Jean Jacques Rousseau, *Discourse upon the Origins and Foundations of Inequality* (Boston: Harvard University, 1950); Sigmund Freud, *Civilization and its Discontents*, tr. James Strachey (New York: W.W. Norton, 1961); John Rawls, *A Theory of Justice* (Cambridge, MA: Harvard, 1971).

12. John Rawls, *A Theory of Justice* (Cambridge, MA: Harvard, 1971).

13. Etienne Gilson, *The Spirit of Mediaeval Philosophy* (Notre Dame, IN: University of Notre Dame, 1991), p. 272.

14. Saint Augustine, *The Confessions*, tr. by Maria Boulding, O.S.B. (New York: Vintage Books, 1998), p. 241.

15. Ibid, p. 172.

16. *Ibid*, p. 178.

17. Cited in Gilson, *The Spirit of Mediaeval Philosophy*, p. 272.

18. *Ibid*, p. 272.

19. *Ibid*, p. 272.

20. G.K. Chesterton, *Orthodoxy* (New York: Doubleday, 1959), p. 169.

21. Peter Kreeft, "Happiness: Ancient and Modern Concepts of Happiness," Catholic Education Resources Council, downloaded 7/24/12; http://www.catholiceducation.org/articles/philosophy/ph0086.htm.

22. *Ibid.*

23. *Ibid.*

24. *Ibid.*

25. *Ibid.*

26. *Ibid.* Kreeft extends the point recalling our identification of sexual decadence and intellectual poverty:

Surely there is an intimate connection between the impurity of the desires of most modern students and the impurity of their motivation for education; between the decline of the sexual love of the other for the other, and of the intellectual love of the truth for the truth; a connection between the contemplative wonder and respect towards the body's mate, and the contemplative wonder and respect towards the mind's mate, truth. To love truth primarily for itself is one thing; to love it primarily for your own sake, for some further utilitarian, instrumental, pragmatic, personal end, is another thing. That is a form of impurity of heart, a sort of intellectual prostitution. And it has cursed modern philosophy ever since Bacon.

27. *Ibid.*

28. Chesterton, *Orthodoxy*, p. 170.

29. http://www.theworkofgod.org/Devotns/Euchrist/holy_eucharist.asp?psearch=Fulton.

30. *Ibid*, p. 153. Feser goes on to observe, interestingly, that "This is one reason secularists are often totally obsessed with politics and prone to utopian fantasies. They do not see any hope for a world beyond this one…and thus insist that heaven, or some reasonable facsimile, simply

must be possible here and now if only we hit upon the right socio-economic-political structures" (p. 153).

Chapter Four

The Ache of Work

What is the connection between a man's work and his life?

Pope John Paul II gives a clear answer in his encyclical letter on human work, *Laborem Exercens*: "Man is made to be in the visible universe an image and likeness of God Himself, and he is placed in it in order to subdue the earth."[1] From the beginning therefore he is called to work, and by his work he is called to be the image God. This means that no matter what the work happens to be, no matter what its objective contents, the subject of work and its fundamental purpose is man himself. By God's design, if not always realized by man, work is for man rather than man for work. Thus the true human good of work is to judge by "the measure of dignity of … the individual who carries it out."[2]

Human work then is not a sentence or enslavement, but is a vocation; a means whereby we take part in God's ongoing Creation as an instrument of His will. Again, according to John Paul II: "Work is a good thing for man—a good thing for his humanity—because through work man *not only transforms nature*, adapting it to his own needs, but he also *achieves fulfillment* as a human being and indeed, in a sense, becomes more a human being."[3] We are the only animal that "works" because work is how we fulfill God's unique plan for us by becoming His image and likeness. As the psychologist Sigmund Freud somewhere said, "There is only work and love." But in so saying, he was just right enough to be dangerously wrong. While there is love and work, they are *not* the only things. The only thing is God, Who is the source and reason for our love and for our work.

It is a cocktail party banality, rarely true, that we are what we do. Too often we are less than what we do. Work can be an opportunity for being, as when theologian Etienne Gilson remarks that: "The plays of Shakespeare, the comedies of Moliere, the symphonies of Beethoven are Shakespeare, Moliere, Beethoven; so much so that we might reasonably ask whether they do not constitute the best part of their authors' being, the very summit of their personality."[4] But more often work is an impediment to being. Thus about work we cannot be indifferent; either it leads to God, which is our heart's desire, or it leads from God, which is hell on earth. At work our lives are in the balance.

BEING IN RETROSPECT

The history of work, like many human histories, traces an arc of rise and fall. Sad to say, its late history, since the industrial revolution, has been mostly fall.

In the pre-capitalist guild systems of medieval Europe one did not work to make money, one worked to make things for other people to use. Work was for the goods needed to make a life with others. With the invention of money economy of the Renaissance came the capitalist middle-man who bought and sold goods and who valued them because they could be exchanged at a profit. In this new market-based system, as Peter Maurin points out, the consumer might never know the producer and the producer might never think of the consumer except as an opportunity for profit.[5] With Enlightenment Protestantism—and that of John Calvin especially—capitalism was given a religious justification. Among the Puritans of early America, personal wealth came to be seen as a blessing by God, as a sign of one's destination in His Kingdom. Where once it was a blessing to be poor ("blessed are the poor in spirit"), it was now a blessing to be wealthy. The motive of self-interest described by Adam Smith came to be seen as a religious value and even a duty. With Protestantism came also the idea of banking and the practice of lending money at interest. Money went from being "merely" a means of exchange to being a means to exact rents from the work of others. Work that had before been the worker's own came to be owned by the banker and his investors. With the industrialization of the 18th and 19th century came factory work in which work was subdivided between man and machine and in which the opportunities of the former were increasingly subject to the logic of the latter. What had before been craft work in which workers wielded their own tools for their own purposes was transformed into assembly-line work in which common tools and gargantuan machines dwarfed worker intents and purposes. And with large-scale manufacturing came the bureaucratization of business organizations in which was born a new class of salaried "managers" whose job it was to seek greater productivity and efficiency through rational scientific control of the work process. As a result, much of the creativity and thought that had before belonged to workers was appropriated by managers and machines. And spurred by endless advances in machine technology, this dehumanizing process has not abated but has continued to exile workers from the most human elements of their work. Today, as digital technology reaches into the finest details of work, there is less work for people to do that cannot be done more efficiently and with higher quality by machines.

In his sobering book entitled *The End of the Modern World*, theologian Romano Guardini traces what this historical transformation of the processes and products of work has meant for the worker:

> The handicrafts, on which all preceding culture was based, are disappearing. As the machine is perfected, the intimate relation of man to his work, in which his eye, hand, will, sense of material, imagination, and general creativeness cooperate, disappears. Process and product alike become ever farther removed from intellectual-physical norms and forces. They are founded on scientific knowledge and the practicalities of construction, and effected by mechanical processes.
>
> As a result, in some respects, man himself grows poorer. He loses the rich satisfaction of personal creativity, consenting instead to invent, utilize, and service mechanical contraptions. But even as he puts them to ever more varied tasks, gaining through them ever greater power, his own will and creativeness must conform ever more to the mechanism in question, for one-sided effects do not exist. This means that the producer renounces individuality in his product and learns to content himself with producing only what the machine allows. The more perfect the apparatus, the fewer the possibilities for personal creativeness. And along with diminishing creativity, the human element, which lives so strongly in work made by hand is also lost. In place of the artisan we have the worker, servicer of machines. For the customer too, something is lost, the personal contact with things that is possible only between persons and personally created objects. The customer is reduced to the modern consumer whose tastes are dictated by mass production, advertising, and sales techniques. And this to the point where he comes to consider the standards and values which only genuine craftsmanship can satisfy as senseless or effete.[6]

The story of diminished being at work is poignant when told in person. An example comes from autoworker, Ben Hamper, who chronicled his experience working the "rivet line" in the General Motors bus and truck assembly plant in Flint, Michigan. Here he describes his greatest challenge at work:

> ...the age old plight that came to haunt every screw jockey: what the [*expletive deleted*] do you do to kill the clock? There were ways of handling nimwit supervisors and banana sticker rednecks and lopsided rails. But the clock was a whole different mammal altogether: It sucked on you as you awaited the next job. It ridiculed you each time you'd take a peek. The more irritated you became, the slower it moved. The slower it moved the more you thought. Thinking was a very slow death at times.
>
> Desperation led me to all the usual dreary tactics used to fight back the clock. Boring excursions like racing to the water fountain and back, chain-smoking, feeding Chee-tos to mice, skeet shooting Milk Duds with rubber

bands, punting washers into the rafter high above the train depot, spitting contests. Any method was viable just as long as it was able to evaporate one more stubborn minute.[7]

Such is the monotony of work in which "every minute, every hour, every truck and every movement was a plodding replica of the one that had gone before."[8]

A theatrical account of diminished being at work comes from playwright Arthur Miller in his modern classic *Death of a Salesman*. In this scene, Willy Loman's two grown sons, Biff and Happy, who have returned home for a stay and who have retired to their boyhood bedroom, talk of their early adult work lives:[9]

HAPPY: But I think if you just got started—I mean—is there any future for you out there?

BIFF: I tell ya, Hap, I don't know what the future is. I don't know—what I'm supposed to want.

HAPPY: What do you mean?

BIFF: Well, I spent six or seven years after high school trying to work myself up. Shipping clerk, salesman, business of one kind or another. And it's a measly manner of existence. To get on that subway on the hot mornings in summer. To devote your whole life to keeping stock, or making phone calls, or selling or buying. To suffer fifty weeks of the year for the sake of a two-week vacation, when all you really desire is to be outdoors, with your shirt off. And always to have to get ahead of the next fella. And still—that's how you build a future. …

HAPPY: You're a poet, you know that, Biff? You're a—you're an idealist!

BIFF: No, I'm mixed up very bad. Maybe I oughta get married. Maybe I ought get stuck into something. Maybe that's my trouble. I'm like a boy. I'm not married, I'm not in business, I just—I'm like a boy.

Such is the emptiness of work that has only worldly meaning. Answering Biff's further lament that "I've always made a point of not wasting my life, and every time I come back here I know that all I've done is to waste my life," Happy exclaims in kind that "I don't know what the hell I'm workin' for."

And finally, a perhaps surprising account of diminished "being" comes from one who, by any worldly measure and certainly by the reckoning of

Willy Loman's two sons, has "made it" in the world. Popular writer Michael Lewis came on the scene with a tale of his life as a bond salesman on Wall Street in the 1980's working for the white-shoe investment bank Salomon Brothers. His account begins with the disclaimer that he wrote it, not as a bitterly estranged worker seeking revenge on his employer, but as a successful up-and-comer:

> It should be said that I was, by the standards we use to measure ourselves, a success. I made a lot of money. I was told often by people who ran our firm that I would one day join them at the top. I would rather not make this boast early. But the reader needs to know that I have been given no reason to feel bitterly toward or estranged from my former employer. I set out to write this book only because I thought it would be better to tell the story than to go on living the story. [10]

The story, as Lewis tells it, was one of moral jeopardy in which he was to do whatever was necessary to make money for the firm. Here he relates how after a few months on a new assignment he learned to regard his clients, not as customers to be served, but as tools for the firm's avarice.

> Now I admit, even for a geek, it was a little embarrassing to let investors believe their white magic. But as long as the chartists placed their bets with me, my jungle guide explained, the reasoning of our customers was not for me to question. Just the opposite. Only days after landing my new post I found myself praising such statements from investors as "I was looking at the ten-day moving average last night and it is a perfect reverse duck tail and pheasant. Let's bet the ranch." At this juncture my role was only to shout encouragement: Yeah! Do it!
>
> In need of a euphemism for what we did with other people's money, we called it arbitrage, which was just plain obfuscation. *Arbitrage* means "trading risklessly for profit." Our investors always took risk: *high-wire act* would have been more accurate than *arbitrage*. In spite of the responsibility implied by my job, I was ignorant and malleable when I advised my first customers. I was an amateur pharmacologist, prescribing drugs without a license. The people who suffered as a result were, of course, my customers. [11]

Later, with a little more time on the job and a lot more perspective, Lewis could see clearly how the game was played:

> Who do you work for? That question haunted salesmen. When a trader screwed a customer and the salesman became upset, the trader would ask the salesman, "Who do you work for anyway?" The message was clear: You work for Salomon Brothers. You work for me. I pay your bonus at the end of the year. So just shut up, you geek. All of which was true, as far as it went. But if you stood back and looked at our business, this was a ridiculous attitude. A policy of screwing investors could lead to ruin. If they ever caught on, we'd have no investors. Without investors, we'd have no business raising money.

The only justification—if you can call it that—that I ever heard for our policy came unwittingly from our president, Tom Strauss, himself a former salesman of government bonds. At a lunch with one of my customers, apropos of nothing and everything, he offered this opinion: "Customers have very short memories." If that was the guiding principle of Salomon Brothers in the department of customer relations, then all was suddenly clear. Screw'em, they'll eventually forget about it! Right. [12]

Such is the depravity of work that reaches to no end higher than making money; a depravity seen on Wall Street many times before and many times since.

And so, in many walks of life, we struggle to "be." We ache for work in which we can take part in God's creation and not be handed-over to the purposes of others; work in which we are not, either directly as workers or indirectly as consumers, a means to the worldly end of making money. As Pope John Paul II notes, ours is the alienation of work:

...organized so as to ensure maximum returns and profits with no concern whether the worker, through his own labor, grows or diminishes as a person, either through increased sharing in a genuinely supportive community or through increased isolation in a maze of relationships marked by destructive competitiveness and estrangement, in which he is considered only a means and not an end. [13]

And so "being" at work is a problem. We want to be found, yet we are lost. We want to be whole, yet we are in pieces. We want to be perfect, yet we are full of faults. We want to love and be loved, yet we are closed-off. We want to be at peace, yet we are troubled by anxieties. Ours is a hunger we can never quite satisfy at work. We join the team, strive to do great things, submit to bosses, and scurry to pile up money, power, adulation, and achievement. We ache of a being that never quite comes, no matter our station in life or standard of living.

BEING DENIED

If the human question at work is "To be or not to be?" it seems that too often the answer is "not to be." Too often work stifles the human spirit. [14] Calling to mind the lessons of earlier chapters we can now see when and how this happens. Work impoverishes when it denies our divinity, when it affirms that we are for science to say, when it denies that we are in communion, when it denies that we are male and female in one flesh, when it denies that we are contingent, and when it denies that we are each unto ourselves.

We Are Divine

As we saw in Chapter 2, we take part in God's divinity—not only His being but also His virtues of unity, indivisibility, eternity, intelligence, freedom, truth, beauty and good. Work cannot but impoverish our being when it treats us, not as would-be divinity but as instrument of worldly purpose, and not as subject and purpose of work but as object and factor of production. As described in Chapter 3, this is the cast of modern mind that regards things as objects and not as beings. When a person is regarded this way—as a reified entity instead of as the image and likeness of God—his material actuality is the focus rather than his personality. As noted by John Paul II, dehumanization results when:

> ...the scale of values is reversed and "productivism" becomes the only parameter of the industrial phenomenon, when the interior dimension of values is neglected, when the aim pursued is rather the perfection of the work than the perfection of the one who carries it out, giving preference in this way to the work as compared with the worker, the object, as compared to the subject.[15]

Such objectification is the basis of economist Karl Marx's famous critique of the capitalist mode of production which regards the worker as a commodity and factor of production and thereby estranges him from his own nature.[16] It is also the basis of what psychoanalyst Ernest Schachtel describes as the "alienated identity" and which he attributes to modern industrialization:

> "The question [of identity] ... has haunted many people increasingly in the last hundred years. They no longer feel certain who they are because in modern industrial society, as Hegel and Marx first showed, they are alienated from nature, alienated from their fellow men, alienated from the work of their hands and minds, and alienated from themselves. I can only state here my belief that self-alienation, the doubt about and search for identity, always goes together with alienation from others and from the world around us."[17]

In more specific terms, work can rob workers of being by turning them from the beatitudes that lead to God. Thus, where Jesus taught that "blessed are the poor in spirit, for theirs is the kingdom of God" we can ask how often work to the contrary calls for a materialism in which "the good life" is having things and a consumerism in which the fun of life is acquiring things?[18] Where Jesus taught that "blessed are those who mourn, for they shall be comforted," we can ask how often work to the contrary advertises a life that is easy and carefree, soft and luxurious, and free from pain, suffering, and inconvenience?[19] Where Jesus taught that "blessed are the meek, for they shall inherit the earth," we can ask how often work to the contrary applauds conquest in competitions to ruin competitors?[20] Where Jesus taught that "blessed are those who hunger and thirst for righteousness, for they shall be filled," we can ask how often work to the contrary calls for self-interest and "looking out for number one"? Where Jesus taught that "blessed are the merciful, for they shall obtain mercy," we can ask how often work to the contrary compares itself to war, celebrates a "take no prisoners" attitude, and counsels taking but not giving advantages and opportunities? Where Jesus taught that "blessed are the pure in heart, for they shall see God," we can ask how often work to the contrary is given to production and consumption of products contrary to the health and dignity of human persons—trade in drugs, alcohol, pornography, guns, violent video games, and needless cosmetic surgery, to name a few? Where Jesus taught that "blessed are the peacemakers, for they shall be called sons of God," we can ask how often work to the contrary seeks profits in armed conflicts or in the fear of such. And, where Jesus taught that "blessed are those persecuted for righteousness' sake, for theirs is the kingdom of heaven," we can ask how often work to the contrary ignores or undermines righteousness by forsaking profit-reducing religious beliefs and practices such as Sabbath restrictions on commerce and travel or "blue-laws" regarding sales of alcohol?[21]

We Are Not for Science to Say

Modern business adheres to the premise attributed to psychologist Kurt Lewin that "there is nothing so practical as a good theory."[22] More hopeful than true, this premise justifies most business education today. Thus a typical introductory course teaches students to be managers by equipping them with scientific theories of motivation, decision-making, work design, communication, persuasion, group dynamics, social networks, leadership, ethics, organization structure, managerial control systems, culture, managing change, and so on. Students are led to think of workers as a factor of production like capital or raw materials, literally as a "resource" to put to business purposes. And so students imagine that business management is an expertise of using scientific theories to put people to productive use. How to do this they cannot say, as they know not how to go from theory to practice.

The idea of using science to manage people is famously identified with Fredrick Taylor, the father of so-called "scientific management," and it is epitomized by his "task idea":

> Perhaps the most prominent single element in modern scientific management is the task idea. The work of every workman is fully planned out by the management at least one day in advance, and each man receives in most cases complete written instructions, describing in detail the task which he is to accomplish, as well as the means to be used in the doing of the work. And the work planned in advance in this way constitutes a task which is to be solved, not by the workman alone, but in almost all cases by the joint effort of the

workman and the management. This task specifies not only what is to be done, but how it is to be done and the exact time. [23]

That such thinking can rob workers of being is easy to see. A case in point is described in a Harvard Business School study of the NASA Skylab Program. Set in the early 1970's, the case centers upon the work of three United States astronauts on their 84 day mission aboard the US Skylab space station. In an instance of scientific management writ large, the crew's work was planned in precise detail and to the minute by NASA engineers, and the crew's every action was closely monitored and checked against the plan by NASA flight control engineers at Mission Control in Houston. Having implemented Taylor's "task idea" to a 'T,' the engineers regarded the astronauts as they regarded all the other devices on the spacecraft; that is, as finely calibrated machines to deploy at will. As described by the case writer: "Skylab had been designed by engineers and technical people who were largely oblivious to the physical needs and limitations—far less comforts—of its future human inhabitants." [24] Moreover, "mission control scheduled the astronauts as tightly as possible. They prided themselves on knowing more than the crew did about how their time could and should be used." [25] As the Flight Director, Neil Hutchinson put it:

> We could have planned a guy's day without leaving a spare minute if we wanted to—we had that ability. We prided ourselves here that from the time the men got up to the time they went to bed, we had every minute programmed...You know, we really controlled their destiny. [26]

However, as the Skylab 3 mission unfolded, the astronauts proved not to be the predictable machines of the engineers' fancy and soon drove the engineers to exasperated aggravation by fumbling with expensive equipment, falling behind schedule, ruining key experiments, and at bitter length turning-off the radio and mounting a strike. The astronauts declared that they could not and would not bear the insult of their work to their being. What they needed and wanted was freedom and time enough to be themselves. As Skylab 3 Flight Commander Gerald Carr put it:

> People in our line of work...very technical work...are inclined to move along with blinders on. You begin to get so involved with details...that you forget to look around you...I think a crew or any man who is working long hours needs some period of time...where he can be quiet and wind down in order to get a good night's sleep. You make less mistakes. You are much more creative, I think, when you are healthy and alert...it's just necessary that a guy have an opportunity...to just stare out the window and gather (his) thoughts. [27]

We Are in Communion

As shown in Chapter 1 we have more or less being as we are more or less in communion with others in God. Such communion, we observed, does not absorb our being, but values and preserves it in a relation of one totality to another.

Work can deny being by disrupting communion in God in various ways. For one, its design can limit meaningful contacts among workers. This is a lesson of the Tavistock coal mining studies in which coal miners flourished when assigned to work as "mates" in small groups for equal wages on tasks that granted to them personal autonomy and called from them adaptability to one another, but became disheartened, depressed, and resentful when assigned to methods of coal extraction which left them no autonomy and kept them from meaningful interactions as equals.[28] For another, work can keep workers from sharing their faith and thereby their communion in God. Such is the "political correctness" that keeps the most important things from public discussion. For a third, work can disrupt communion, not by separating people, but by denying them the privacy necessary to preserve their integrity as persons. This is a dilemma of many so-called "open offices" in which employees are located in common work spaces and encouraged to interact at every opportunity. As psychologist Susan Cain has recently observed, this is a problem especially for introverts who more are sensitive to interruptions in their work and who prefer to work apart from others in quieter settings.[29] But what is true of introverts in typical circumstances may be true of extroverts at the extremes.

Lately, work has invented a new way to disrupt communion, by putting it online. Work interactions that were conducted face-to-face in person, or ear-to-ear by phone, can be conducted screen-to-screen in "virtual reality" (an oxymoron if ever there was). In this last, virtual persons know one another by self-styled digital "profiles" (that may profile fiction as well as fact), come together in virtual spaces such as Facebook or LinkedIn, and interact asynchronously as convenient or not at all. Champions of this brave new world proclaim that it opens-up new possibilities of communion freed from entanglements of time, space, and body. But in fact it denies the very possibility of human communion which depends upon the full engagement of persons in body and spirit. What makes a person a person is just his composite of body and soul, and what makes a communion a communion is just its congress of bodies and souls. As many have lately noted, people who interact through computer screens have neither the vulnerability nor responsibility required for true friendship.[30] And when such ersatz interactions are not relieved by contact in real friendship people become commodities to one another—objects of perhaps fetishistic attention—and thereby become alienated from one another. Here is philosopher Roger Scruton:

You "click on" your friend, as you might click on a news item or a music video. He is one of the many products on display. Friendship with him, and relationships generally, belong in the category of amusements and distractions, a commodity that may be chosen, or not, depending on the rival goods. This contributes to a radical demotion of the personal relationship. *Your friendships are no longer special to you and definitive of your moral life: they are amusements, things that have no real life of their own.* "[31]

There is a difference, Scruton observes, between "the true freedom that comes through relationships with other subjects and the hidden enslavement that comes when our outward ventures are not towards subjects but towards objects." Recalling Marx and Hegel, he concludes that: "We must distinguish the *realization* of the self, in free relations with others, from the *alienation* of the self in the system of things."[32]

We Are Male and Female in "One Flesh"

We have seen that human being is nuptial—that the capacity for reason that sets man apart from the animals arises from the spiritual union of male and female in God's image. This capacity, we have seen, is created in the nuptial acts of love, play and fulfillment.

Work can deny being by separating the male and female spirits that comprise the nuptial image of God. This it can do either by standardizing work inputs to require no feminine receptivity or accommodation (inputs in which each is, in the words of Ben Hamper, "a plodding replica of the one that had gone before"), or by standardizing work outputs to require no masculine initiative or creativity. In general, whenever workers are kept from thinking and acting for themselves, they are kept from becoming complete and integrated human persons. This inhuman prospect of dispiriting work has long been a concern of the Catholic Church, as Pope John Paul II emphasizes in his encyclical on human work, *Laborem Exercens*:

> Every effort must be made to ensure that in this kind of system also the human person can preserve his awareness of working "for himself." If this is not done, incalculable damage is inevitably done throughout the economic process, not only economic damage but first and foremost damage to man.[33]

Of this "incalculable damage" let us add the further detail that it occurs as workers are kept from the nuptial acts of love, play, and fulfillment by which they come into God. Where love is a meeting of male initiative and female receptivity, a machine or manager can preempt one or both. Where play is a meeting of male invention and female realism, a machine or manager can sacrifice one or both to programmed routine. And where fulfillment is a meeting of male truth and female possibility, a machine or manager can hide one or both.

Work can deny being in a more basic way, by failing to support the family which is the most crucial nuptial image of God. As the Church points out in her *Catechism*:

> The family is the *original cell of social life*. It is the natural society in which husband and wife are called to give themselves in love and in the gift of life. Authority, stability, and a life of relationships with the family constitute the foundations for freedom, security, and fraternity within society.[34]

Work undermines the family when it fails to provide workers just remuneration, where "just remuneration," explains John Paul II, is that necessary "for establishing and properly maintaining a family and for providing security for its future."[35] Too many employers today fail their workers in this way, often with the lame excuse (that excuses nothing) that they are paying workers the market rate.

Finally, work can contribute to a wider culture that ignores, neglects, or denies the nuptial foundation of human being. More and more it is said that there are no differences between man and woman that make any difference; no reciprocity that defines a whole that includes and is greater than both. Where 'sexual equality' used to mean that men and women have different but equally important roles to play in society, today it means that men and women have the same roles to play in society. And, where 'marriage' used to mean the union of a man and a woman, today it means the union of any two adults, male or female. Such rejection of bodily and cultural differences between male and female cannot but come at the expense of the spiritual differences that unite male and female in the image of God. And so we cannot be surprised by mounting losses to our being in God. On the university campus an unwillingness to confine sexual relations to a man and woman in marriage has arisen alongside an inability to think critically and reason well about the world.[36] And in the wider culture the so-called sexual revolution (with its sensational ideas and valuation of non-nuptial sexuality) has arisen alongside a general decay and coarsening of culture. These are parallel signs of failing the nuptial compact with God. That these signs are missed or misunderstood may be the greatest impediment today to our being fully in God, at work or anywhere else.

We Are Contingent

The worst that work can do is to deny the possibility of being in God. It was this that Arthur Miller's characters Biff and Happy Loman couldn't imagine (as they had no idea of what it is to "be" in the world); that Ben Hamper at G.M. couldn't manage (as he couldn't escape the "here and now" of the time clock); and that Michael Lewis couldn't ignore (as he thought it better to tell his story rather than go on living it—or rather dying in it).

The tragedy in every failure to be is that it is unnecessary. It is for us to make the bed in which we lay, to decide whether and how we will be by whether and how we relate to God. Nevertheless, work can blind us to this possibility and this responsibility by calling us to other possibilities and responsibilities. It may command or beguile with its own "hero system" which calls not for being in God but for lesser worldly goods. It may offer laurels and cash money to bright-eyed and savvy "winners" who are happy to do its bidding, even and especially when that bidding leads away from God by paying the lowest possible wage to employees, or taking advantage of a natural disaster to gouge customers for necessities, or awarding triple-A ratings to toxic securities to sell them at a premium, or overlooking so-called "externalities" such depleting scarce resources or of polluting the environment.

With or without our conscious complicity, we can spend the better part of a life not seeing our contingency of being. But see we may in what we jokingly refer to as the mid-life crisis (jokingly because we know no other way to face its existential challenge than to laugh). And so in middle-age we wake up one day to discover that our work has no life and no soul, and that our frantic claims to "meaning" and "achievement" are empty.[37] Then at last we see the tragic arc of our work; that we have authored our undoing as our once hopeful enthusiasm of youth reached to a climax of middle-life achievement and prosperity only to end in an old-age in rue of a life squandered. Our middle life crisis is more than a cliché; it is a belated but hopefully not too late recognition of the futility of work without God.

We Are Each unto Ourselves

Although work is an opportunity to be, there is always more to being a person than any job or role or position in society. Whereas a job is a material process in space and time, a person, as we saw in chapter 1, is an integral spirit beyond space and time. Whereas a job has parts and has an end, a person has no parts and has no end. And whereas the logic of a job concerns whether it is productive and efficient, the logic of a person concerns whether he finds love, play, and fulfillment in God. Thus, and as we've seen, work can impoverish being when it compels the worker to conform to it rather than it conforming to the worker. Machine or management control over work represses the spontaneity needed to be humanly present to work and to other persons. As John Paul II points out:

> Machines, with their rigid automatism, are unrewarding and offer little satisfaction. The very relations between fellow workers, when they become deper-

sonalized, cannot give the necessary comfort or support; and the machinery of production, distribution, and consumption often forces workers to live in a "standardized" way, without initiatives, without choices.[38]

As work and worker are incommensurate, the latter should never be mistaken for the former. And yet, how often are workers seen only in terms the work they do? This is to subject their supernatural spirit, which is immaterial, timeless, and absolutely unique to an artificial regime, which is material, time-bound, and often routine. And this is to mistake their being, which is the far greater thing, for a job, which is the far lesser thing. Cruel and senseless as it is to think of people this way, we do so all the time, at work as we've seen, and even at leisure as when we ask a person about their job thinking thereby that we have asked about their person. Indeed, we hardly notice the chill of the question; that in the asking we have made the person less than they are and can be.

BE-COMING AND BE-GOING AT WORK

When we step back to look at business in the large, we see how it can rob us of being by confounding our purpose. Business can size us up as it sizes up all things, with bottom-line questions such as: "Does it "work"? "Will it sell? And above all, "Will it make money?" When industrialist Alfred P. Sloan declared the business of business to be business, he identified business with the largely American philosophy of pragmatism that judges all things by the difference it makes to accept them; i.e., by whether and how well they "work." Pragmatism is the counsel to put ends before means, to put worldly consequences before spiritual first principles. Its method, according to philosopher William James, is to identify the "cash value" of an idea as a condition for accepting it.[39] Thus business can take us from God by finding our good not in what God makes, but in the money we make. And because it is not possible to honor God and Mammon at the same time, business can ask us to abandon the one for the other, or at least observe the one on Sunday and the other on other days.

To put the pragmatism of business before the truth of God is thus a sure way to lose our way in the world, a sure way to go out of being. Again, there is but one becoming in life—one authentic and true purpose—and that is to become in God. To see this is to see that our human purposes are not all equal in being but must be ordered according to their reach to God. Even a single act can have various consequences for being. The story is told of Sir Christopher Wren, the designer of St. Paul's Cathedral in London, who would sometimes wander the construction site and without announcing himself ask the stone masons what they were doing. One spoke of his work as a "job;" a market exchange of labor for pay. Another spoke of his work as a "career;" a step on the path of his personal development. But a third spoke of his work by gesturing toward the heavens and saying something along the lines of: "I am helping God and Sir Christopher Wren build this beautiful cathedral." Of the three we can and must ask: "Who has more being at work?"

And so, as we long for work that calls upon and develops our human personality—for work that expresses our God-given gifts, talents, and virtues—it is not enough for us to be at work, we must be in God at work. God is the source and fulfillment of our being. Too often we pursue work for its own sake or for a sake other than God's. Such is the disease of the "workaholic" who finds that no matter how much work he accomplishes he is never fulfilled. He puts work in place of God who is his heart's true desire. He does not see, with St. Augustine, that his heart will not rest until it rests in Him. At work therefore, our question is Shakespeare's: "To be or not to be?" We are more or less; mostly less it seems. And of us there can always be more; much more it seems. Perhaps if we are clearer about the question of being we can have more rather than less.

NOTES

1. John Paul II, Encyclical letter *On Human Work: Laborem Exercens* (Boston, MA: Pauline Books, 1981), p. 5.

2. *Ibid*, p. 17.

3. *Ibid*, p. 23.

4. Etienne Gilson, *Spirit of Mediaeval Philosophy*, p. 89.

5. Peter Maurin, *Easy Essays* (Eugene, OR: Wipf & Stock, 2003), p. 80.

6. Roman Guardini, *The End of the Modern World* (Wilmington, DL: ISI Books, 1998), pp. 155-156.

7. Ben Hamper, *Rivethead* (New York: Warner Books, 1991), p. 95.

8. *Ibid*, 41.

9. Arthur Miller, *Death of a Salesman*, Text and Criticism, edited by G. Weales (New York: The Viking Press, 1967, pp. 22-23.

10. Michael Lewis, *Liar's Poker* (New York: Penguin Books, 1989), p. 9.

11. *Ibid*, p. 163.

12. *Ibid*, p. 167.

13. John Paul II, Encyclical letter *Centesimus Annus*, 5/1/1991; http://www.vatican.va/holy_father/john_p.

14. A crude but suggestive indication of the state of being at work is self-reported satisfaction at work. Barely 45% of Americans are satisfied with their jobs, a figure which has been on the decline over the last several decades, c.f., Ferdinand Tablan, "Human alienation and fulfillment in work: Insights from the Catholic social teachings, *Journal of Religion and Business Ethics*, http://via.library.depaul.edu/jrbe/vol3/iss5.

15. John Paul II, Address to the Christian Union of Entrepreneurs and Managers, *L'Osservatore Romano*, December 24, 1979, p. 3.

16. Karl Marx, "Economic and philosophic manuscripts of 1844," in The Marx-Engels Reader, ed. Robert Tucker (New York: W.W. Norton and Company, 1972), p. 78.

17. Ernest G. Schachtel, "On alienated concepts of identity," *American Journal of Psychoanalysis, 41*(2), pp. 120-127, 1961.

18. How much of advertising, fashion, and planned obsolescence is to spur demand for things people don't need? And what precisely is the nobility in persuading people that the

meaning of life is to find, not in the being of God, but in having a late-model sports car? The "poor in spirit" are those who, regardless of their wealth or place in society, know the good of being without either. Knowing that being lies not in "having" but in "giving," they do not give themselves up to any purely human plan for reality—such as fame or fortune—but give themselves up to God's plan for reality—which is to love God above all things and to love neighbor as self.

19. Ease sells Maytag washing machines; luxury sells BMW automobiles; and freedom from suffering and inconvenience sells pharmaceuticals, alcohol and recreational drugs, cosmetics, and home delivery of all things under the sun. By contrast, those who mourn, who know the inner discontent and suffering of not living up to what they can be, know thereby to look beyond to God who, in the person of Jesus Christ, gives victory to love over hate, joy over pain, and life over death.

20. The meek are not competitive in this way and do not seek to harm because they know both that the best things are spiritual not material and that spiritual things are not exclusive but multiply when shared.

21. A visible exception that perhaps proves this rule about business today is the fast-food chain *Chick-fil-A* which shutters its 1615 locations every Sunday in observance of the Sabbath at the expense of a not insignificant percentage of its potential profits.

22. See Lloyd Sandelands, "What is so practical about theory: Lewin revisited," Journal *for the Theory of Social Behavior, 20(3)*, pp. 357-379.

23. Fredrick Taylor, *Scientific Management* (New York: Harper & Row, 1947), p. 39.

24. E. Mary Lou Balbaky & Michael B. McCaskey, *Strike in space* (Boston, MA: Harvard Business School, 1980); 9-481-008, p. 10.

25. *Ibid*, p. 11.

26. *Ibid*, p. 11.

27. *Ibid*, p. 16.

28. Eric Trist & William Bamforth," Some social and psychological consequences of the long wall method of coal-getting," *Human Relations*, 4, 3-38, 1951.

29. Susan Cain, *Quiet: The power of introverts in a world that can't stop talking* (New York: Crown, 2012).

30. See for examples: Roger Scruton, "Hiding behind the screen," *The New Atlantis*, Summer 2010; Sherry Turkel, *Alone Together: Why We Expect More from Technology and Less from Each Other* (New York: Basic Books, 2012); Andrew Reiner, "Only disconnect," *The Chronicle of Higher Education*, September 24, 2012.

31. Roger Scruton, "Hiding behind the screen," p. 51.

32. *Ibid*, p. 54.

33. John Paul II, *Laborem Exercens*, p. 38.

34. *Catechism of the Catholic Church* (New York: Doubleday, 1995), p. 590.

35. John Paul II, *Laborem Exercens*, 46. On a more general level the John Paul concludes that "the whole labor process must be organized and adapted in such a way as to respect the requirements of the person and his or her forms of life, above all life in the home, taking into account the individual's age and sex" (p. 47).

36. For lengthy treatments of this claim see Allan Bloom, *The Closing of the American Mind* (New York: Simon and Schuster, 1988) and Lloyd E. Sandelands, *The Nuptial Mind* (Lanham, MD: University Press of America, 2012).

37. Anthropologist Ernest Becker referred to this problem of meaning as "the main psychoanalytic problem of life," noting the inevitable existential crisis that comes when one becomes aware of what they are doing to earn their self esteem and of the fact that self-esteem is earned only in a societal "hero system" that is culturally and historically arbitrary—see Ernest Becker, *The Denial of Death* (New York: Free Press, 1975).

38. John Paul II, *L'Ossevatore Romano*, p. 3.

39. William James, *Pragmatism* (New York: Prometheus Books, 1991). According to James:

So the universe has always appeared to the natural mind as a kind of enigma, of which the key must be sought in the shape of some illuminating or power-bringing word or name. That word names the universe's principle , and to possess it is after a fashion to possess the universe itself. 'God,' 'Matter,' 'Reason,' 'the Absolute,' 'Energy,' are so many solving names. You can rest when you have them. You are at the end of your metaphysical quest. But if you follow the pragmatic method, you cannot look on any such word as closing your quest. You must bring out of each word its practical cash-value, set it at work within the stream of your experience. It appears less as a solution, then, than as a program for more work, and more particularly as an indication of the ways in which existing realities may be changed.

Chapter Five

Mind the Person

Some 40 years ago, Robert Greenleaf prophesied that business one day would take human being seriously, that it would no longer find its chief reason and good in material profit, but in the growth and development of persons, both customers and employees.

> I have confidence that, after a bit of confusion, a new business ethic will emerge. And the best I can do at this point is to speculate on what that ethic might be. ... Looking at the two major elements, the work and the person, the new ethic, simply but quite completely stated, will be: *The work exists for the person as much as the person exists for the work.* Put another way, the business exists as much to provide meaningful work to the person as it exists to provide a product or service to the customer. [1]
>
> When the business manager who is fully committed to this ethic is asked, "What are you in business for?" the answer may be: "I am in the business of growing people—people who are stronger, healthier, more autonomous, more self-reliant, more competent. Incidentally, we also make and sell at a profit things that people want to buy so we can pay for all this. We play that game hard and well and we are successful by the usual standards, but that is really incidental...
>
> Utopian? No, I don't think so... [2]

Greenleaf's prophecy of person-centered business may not have been realized in his day, but as we will see it is a real possibility, of which there are hints here and there in our day.

In this final chapter of the book we ask what it would mean to take the metaphysical truths described in the first three chapters and lamented in the fourth as a basis for our lives at work. What would it mean to take being at work seriously, as the final cause for which we exist and as the supreme good we must honor and obey in everything we do? And what must business leaders do to nourish that community of persons that is the foundation of our being? We start by imploring business leaders to behold the metaphysics of work so that they might enable workers to come more fully into being. We continue by reminding business leaders that it is for them to promote being at work by putting the first thing first—namely, the human person in God. Then, with a view to our Divine mystery, we urge leaders to think of their work as a sacred ministry to persons rather than as a profane management of human resources. And finally we close with thanks to God that we do not come to be in Him on our own, that He seeks us more than we seek Him, and that He has given us His Church—the "Mystical Body of Christ"—to make straight our path to Him.

To these ends we keep one eye steady on the teachings of the Church, recognizing that her ethical admonitions are more than dogma but also practical instruction for living the best possible life. We want not to neglect the teachings of the Church so as not to squander our possibilities of being. At the same time, we keep our other eye steady on the testimonies of business leaders who, by honoring the teachings of the Church, point toward that "new day" foretold by Greenleaf. Among these leaders are Max De Pree, CEO of Herman Miller, Inc., J. Robert Ouimet, CEO of the Ouimet- Cordon-Bleu-Tomasso Companies, C. William Pollard, CEO of ServiceMaster; Tom Chappell, co-founder and CEO of Tom's of Maine, and Dennis Bakke, co-founder and CEO of the AES Corporation.

BEHOLD WHAT YOU CANNOT SEE

"Sanity," as theologian Frank Sheed reminds us, "does not mean living in the same world as everyone else; it means living in the real world." "Some of the most important elements in the real world," he observes "can be known only by the revelation of God."[3] And the most important element by far is the human person. There is therefore a need in leaders for a spiritual sense; not as an extra "nice" thing but as a guide to the real world. Such a sense is expressed in this way by Tom Chappell of Tom's of Maine:

> By *spirit* or *spiritual*, I mean the part of you that survives when you eliminate your flesh and bones—the part you can't point to but can feel, the part you might describe to someone else as your essential being, your soul. Soul is what connects you to everyone and everything else. It is the sum of all the choices you make. It is where your beliefs and values reside. Soul is at the center of our relationships to others, and for me it is at the center of the business enterprise.[4]

As this book has been at pains to show, the human person is not a natural thing to "see" in the objective terms of science, but is a spiritual thing to "behold" in the light of faith. For all there is to see of persons—their bodies, interactions, social structures and culture—there is yet to know what is greatest in them, what lies beyond space and time, what God has written into them. To objectify workers thus is not only a metaphysical mistake (a mistake about reality), it is a sin against God who wills man to be formed in His image and likeness. In a word, workers are divine and business leaders should address them as they would God Himself. In this, leaders would do well to heed C.S. Lewis' advice to bow before the most ordinary and dreary-seeming person one could meet:

> It is a serious thing to live in a society of possible gods and goddesses, to remember that the dullest and most uninteresting person you talk to may one day be a creature which, if you saw it now, you would be strongly tempted to worship, or else a horror and corruption such as you now meet, if at all, only in a nightmare. ... There are no ordinary people. You have never talked to a mere mortal. ... Next to the Blessed Sacrament itself, your neighbor is the holiest object presented to your senses.[5]

Thus the business leader must think of workers, not as objects or things to see and use—not as abstractions of "personnel" or "factors of production" or "human resources"—but as persons in God, as spiritual beings to behold and cherish. He must rely, not on the scientific vocabulary that dominates business thinking today, but on the metaphysical vocabulary that the Church maintains to this day. The former is the vocabulary of textbooks on business management that depict workers as isolated and self-contained figures;[6] that size, weigh, and index workers by their objective qualities of knowledge, skill, ability, experience and demography; and that describe the leader's job as "human resources management." The latter is the vocabulary of the Church that teaches that workers are human persons, that workers are spiritual beings in communion, and that workers are beings of degree who come into or go out of being, who are less than they can be, who have material, formal, efficient, and final causes, and who are given by a purpose which is to know and love God.

Different Worlds

These two vocabularies open upon different worlds. Human resources management fits objective workers to objective jobs to maximize efficiency and profit; the Church seeks the being of persons to nurture their growth and development. The one "sees" workers in the abstract objectivity of science; the other "beholds" them in the concrete particularity of their image and likeness of God. The one regards workers as "human resources" to deploy as "factors of production;" the other embraces workers as divinities to nourish in their uniqueness and dignity. The difference between these worlds is the focus of the prophetic Robert Greenleaf who reasons that if being is the true aim of work, then the true test of leadership is whether it enables people to come into being. According to Greenleaf:

> The best test, and difficult to administer, is this: Do those served grow as persons? Do they, while being served, become healthier, wiser, freer, more autonomous, more likely themselves to become servants? And, what is the effect on the least privileged in society? Will they benefit or at least not be further deprived?[7]

This is the test applied by ServiceMaster Corporation, as CEO C. William Pollard observes:

> In ServiceMaster, leadership begins with our objectives: To honor God in all we do, To help people develop, To pursue excellence, and To grow profitably. Thus, our role and obligation as leaders involves more than what a person does on the job. We must also be involved in what that person is becoming and how the work environment is contributing to the process.[8]

And this test is an axiom of the Herman Miller Corporation, as its CEO Max De Pree attests:

> Vital organizations don't grant their members authenticity; they acknowledge that people come already wrapped in authentic humanness. When an organization truly acknowledges the *a priori* authenticity of each person and acts accordingly, how many ways open up for people to reach their potential![9]

Different Leaders

These two vocabularies differ in what they demand of a business leader. Where human resources management stresses the leader's knowledge of the human sciences (of relevant models, theories, and empirical findings) as the key condition for success, the Church gives weight to the leader's character. Where the scientifically oriented leader is called to master valid facts and theories about workers, the metaphysically oriented leader is called to know workers as he knows himself. For the latter, and for us in this book, the challenge of being an effective leader is just that of being human. This challenge is not to meet by training in social science; indeed, such training might limit or stunt the learning required. Rather it is to meet only by experience and wisdom in living as a person with others. In leaders there is no substitute for character.

Different Practicalities

Last but not least, these two vocabularies differ in usefulness. Where the abstract vocabulary of human resources management is not easily fit to the concrete particulars of business, the "in the world" vocabulary of the Church is easily fit to practice because it is already concrete and particular. A leader who thinks scientifically about workers as objects in a field of forces does not on that basis know how best to engage and manage any one of them for the good. To the contrary, there is a maddening gulf between what he knows about workers in scientific terms and what he needs to know to take practical advantage of them.[10] This condition is perhaps familiar to any who have taken part in a management training program. Here a business manager, Michael Brown, opines about such in the *Wall Street Journal*:

> … If, as I suggest, most of these programs are good, why do I not become the super-manager of my aspirations? At various times I've learned how to approach my job as a total business system, how to quantify and measure everything, how to plan strategically, how to manage change, how to manage my time, how to get results by motivating others, and umpteen other proven approaches to successful management. … All this leaves me confused as hell. My management instincts have been watered down. I've now been conditioned to stop in the middle of some management activity and try to remember which techniques might apply. The different management techniques seem to meld into an anti-synergistic mixture, in which the sum is less than the totality of its parts.[11]

In contrast, a leader who thinks metaphysically of workers as beings like himself enjoys definite practical advantages. A *first practical advantage* is that he can know for himself (in his own being) where workers are coming from (their formal causes), where they are going to (their final causes), and what aids or prevents them from realizing their possibilities (their efficient causes). This is the mindset of Tom Chappell of Tom's of Maine who shows how by embracing his charges in this way he not only comes to know who they are but on occasion helps hold them in being. Here he describes an employee in crisis:

> A few years ago, I was in a meeting with a top female executive in my company. Suddenly through the door burst another member of my executive committee with a wild look in his eyes. Before we could say a word, he announced that his wife's mother and sister had just been killed in an automobile accident. Before we could respond, he embraced me and began to cry. I held him until his sobbing subsided. Then he was ready to talk, and I simply listened. He talked of the difficulty of reconciling the fact that the night before these people had been in his house and today they were gone. He talked about how close his kids were to their grandmother and aunt about his own love for them all, about his concern for his wife and her father. Coupled with his grief

was his rage over evidence that their deaths had been caused by a car hurtling the wrong way down the turnpike—a drunk driver at the wheel.

He was having trouble making sense of it all, and since we certainly couldn't either, we just listened. Once his emotion was spent, since we were members of the same church, I asked him if he wanted to pray. We joined hands in a circle, the three of us, and I said a few prayers that seemed to comfort him. Throughout the day I kept in touch with him and made sure everyone in the company knew about the funeral. [12]

While this episode is extreme it exemplifies an attitude that appears to inform Chappell's every interaction at work. Here he draws the larger lesson of the example:

If you cannot imagine something like that ever happening in your own company, then you are missing one of the great joys of business life. I love watching sales go off the chart as much as the next CEO, but success is more than high numbers. I understand that business requires a hierarchy, but I can't tell you how much satisfaction I get when certain bits of people's lives—the marriages, the births, the deaths, the loneliness, the addictions, the healing, the parenting—enter the life of the company and dissolve its power structure into a circle of mutual respect, support, and learning.

Our goal at Tom's of Maine is to respect the inherent dignity of each person as well as the job that person does. [13]

A *second practical advantage* for the leader who thinks of others in this metaphysical way is that he is aware of their possibilities—with Aristotle and Aquinas he understands that people are one part actuality and one part potency. There is always more to workers than meets the eye. As beings created in the image and likeness of God, they share His infinite virtues and His infinite dignity. As ServiceMaster CEO E. William Pollard observes:

We are not machines; we are people, with our own fingerprints of personality and potential. Only people, not machines, can respond to the unexpected and surprise the customer with extraordinary performance. Only people can serve; only people can lead; only people can innovate and create; only people can love and hate. ... We know that animals can learn a conditioned response and repeat an established pattern of behavior. But people have the potential to improve upon their knowledge, to modify, to adapt, and to exercise judgment with a framework of moral values. It is not just what we are doing, but what we are becoming in the process that gives us our distinct value and is uniquely human. [14]

After a bit of struggle, Tom Chappell likewise came to the idea that in every worker there are unseen possibilities and that it is his job to help bring them out:

> In an effort to encourage creativity and high performance, Tom's was trying to get away from the traditional business practices of treating employees as inter-changeable "tools" (or as Kant might put it, as "means" rather than "ends" in themselves)—and treat them instead as worthy for what they are and not for their utility...We listened to our employees, talked through their resentment, and this is what we heard: The company was not doing enough to affirm the "gifts" that it already had. Top management had to work harder to reach out to learn more about the skills of its existing employees and explore ways for people to contribute more to the team. [15]

And so business leaders must lead with workers' being in mind striving always to lead them from their fallen condition of sin to their risen condition of destined beatitude. As Jewish philosopher and Holocaust survivor Viktor Frankl observed, man is to know and to treat not according to how he is, but according to how can he can be: "If we take man as he really is, we make him worse. But if we over-estimate him; if we seem to be idealist and are over-estimating, over-rating him...then we promote him to what he really can be." [16]

A *final practical advantage* for the leader who thinks of others in this metaphysical way is that he can know more keenly (again in his own being) that he and they are of a kind, are "brothers." This advantage is perhaps the most significant and demanding because it makes unconscionable any treat-ment of workers that the leader would not want of himself. By it the leader is returned to the justice of the "Golden Rule" and to Robert Greenleaf's idea of the leader, not as manager of human resources, but as servant of persons. This last is the idea endorsed in one way or another by every one of our business practitioners. Here, Dennis Bakke of the AES Corporation reflects:

> The Creation story does not assign people, even leaders, the responsibility of "managing" other people. The Bible says that people are to have dominion over the animals and plants. It encourages humans to act as stewards for the world we live in. It does not, however, encourage us to dominate other people. It never classifies people as "resources." The Bible does endorse leadership. What is the difference? Biblical leadership requires those in authority to serve the people they lead. Leaders do whatever it takes to allow followers to use their talents effectively. [17]

In sum, if there is a word to summarize our first admonition to the lead-er—*to behold what you cannot see*—it is "love." To love those with whom we work is to behold them—to hold them in being by drawing them to our hearts. Again according to Dennis Bakke:

> "Love" is not a word used much in the rough-and-tumble corporate world, perhaps because it sounds soft and sentimental. ... Leaders who create dynam-ic, rewarding, enjoyable workplaces love people. Love is an act of humility

that says, "I need you." Love affirms that the other person is worthy and
important. Most of us know what love demands. I will not dwell long on this
leadership characteristic. As a young person, I learned that one way to spell
love is T-I-M-E. If I love the people who work in my organization, I will
allocate time to be with them. In some organizations there are sanctions
against "fraternizing with subordinates." I believe refraining from forming
friendships or taking time to know and love people does immense damage to
the spirit of everyone in the workplace. [18]

PUT FIRST THINGS FIRST

As we've seen, the thing to behold that we cannot see is our being in God;
and specifically our being in His image and likeness in the oneness of nuptial
union. As we are about to see, this thing to behold is not just *a* thing to
behold, it is *the* thing to behold. It is our supreme good, *the* thing we must
answer to before all others.

The Supreme Good "Is"

There are four points to emphasize about our supreme good of being in God.
The first is that it is no subjectivity or interpretation but rather that it simply
"is." It is the good of God written indelibly into our being that we cannot
erase however unaware of it we may be and however we may fail to fulfill it
by our actions. As J. Robert Ouimet of the Ouimet-Cordon-Blue-Tomasso
Companies observes, this is the truth to which business leaders cannot but
come if they are sincere in their efforts:

> I am certain that if any two or three people responsible for an organization—
> even if they don't believe in anything but are perhaps just searching for greater
> meaning in their lives—if these people are willing to take the time to meet
> together once a month, to sit down for one or two hours at a time and to reflect
> in silence, then they will not be far from God, and God will not be far from
> them. They will be able to put into practice the types of management activities
> that serve man. I am sure that God, who is Love, Father, Son and Spirit, will
> answer them in some way. He will not refuse to walk with them. He will,
> quietly, through the primacy of human dignity, through what is human. And he
> will help them to discover Love. I feel certain that what I say is the truth, for in
> my heart I feel a sustained and constant peace. [19]

The Supreme Good is Nuptial

A second point to emphasize about our supreme good of being in God is that
it is nuptial; it is a meeting and merging of male and female in the oneness of
God. As we saw in Chapter 2, the creative realism that distinguishes man
from all other creatures is a consummation of female and male—of female

empathy, receptivity, and accommodation and male focus, activity, and projection. As we saw in Chapter 3, the integral community that distinguishes human society from animal aggregates (of troop, herd, school, flock, or hive) is the result of nuptial acts of love, play, and fulfillment that again marry male and female in the image and likeness of God. And as we saw in Chapter 4, this reciprocity of male and female is too often ignored or neglected or even repudiated in our lives today.

While he does not put it in explicitly nuptial terms, Tom Chappell understood the creativity of Tom's of Maine as originating in the complementary differences between his wife Kate and himself, differences that are strikingly female and male:

> ...the differences between Kate and me are evident in the history of Tom's of Maine. Kate is the artist of the family, the poet, the chef, the gardener, and somehow she's managed to blend and fuse her talents with me, the visionary, the promoter, the salesman, the organizer, the hard-driver. ... The creative process, the process of imagination, happens when these two contrasting forces come together, each with its own integrity, but each able to give way to the other to form something new. [20]

Indeed, this nuptial imagery runs through Tom Chappell's understanding of his business as the following two examples attest. Here he draws the reader to a conclusion about how a business can achieve a high level of innovativeness by insisting on (female) intuition in the face of (male) rationality:

> The message of this particular experience at Tom's: Let the intuitive guide us all. Creative solutions will follow. Imagination is too sacred to lose. Nurture and respect it. Turbo-charged powerboats and fixed agendas and methods of being keep us from the "feel" of our business. Sail into open waters, and navigate along with the winds and the tides. Allow yourself to get in touch with the insights and creativity—the sacred—around you, and let it guide you. The reason big companies buy small companies is that the giants lose their capacity to be creative and innovative. They are too burdened by rationality and analysis. Let your imagination fly. Trust your intuition. Create opportunities for your managers to be creative. You're already great at crunching numbers. By combining rationality and creativity you can help your company become great. [21]

And here Chappell, again without mentioning the nuptial in so many words, describes the logic of his business as two-fold; as involving both a soft-edged (read female) circle of mutuality and a hard-edged (read male) triangle of hierarchy:

At Tom's of Maine, two different paradigms guide our business style. As I
discussed in chapter 6, the circle is how we gather together to listen to a
problem, to share and listen to opinions, and to function as a team in generat-
ing a new creative solution. The circle is not a place where anyone's personal
agenda is ramrodded through. Your individual responsibility as a member of
the circle is to listen to the others, reflect, and then assert your own point of
view. You facilitate by encouraging another person to say more about their
idea; it's a conversation of people who believe that the outcome will be co-
created.

We also have the triangle, which symbolizes the structure of authority at
Tom's, differentiated by the value of a particular job. A vice-president has a
different job value from a product manager. This kind of hierarchy has nothing
to do with power or creativity; it's simply how decisions get made. In the
course of every decision there is someone at the top of that triangle, an authority on that team.

The circle is there for listening and opennesss, for dialogue and co-creat-
ing; the triangle is there for the structure, to remind everybody of who gets to
make the decision, at every level of the company. ...

And so these two systems, the circle and the triangle, come together into a
different paradigm of doing business, affirming the contribution that everyone
makes to the process but within the tradition of authority. Everyone is equal in
the circle, but someone in the triangle is in charge.[22]

Behind Chappell's thinking about business—thinking that is strikingly male
and female—is an idea shared by all of our exemplary leaders; namely that
their business is a "family." This idea is more than a metaphor or platitude
about "family values." For Chappell, Tom's of Maine is to contrast with the
usual image of business as a rational order:

Businesses have traditionally been organized into a hierarchy of positions that
carry inherent power and authority, from the CEO to the mailroom. Jobs
themselves are organized into different functions—marketing, sales, research
and development, finance, manufacturing, service. The marketplace deter-
mines the relative value of a job. A person's worth is measured by the job he
or she holds and how competent he or she is. The job categories themselves
can have their own hierarchy (for example, manufacturing is typically lower
down on the pole than finance, and service may be perceived as lesser than
marketing).

But many of us in corporate life also have another very different kind of
human association—the family. In the family we learn love, patience, respect,
nurturing, affirmation, and health. The family also teaches us about competition, domination, selfishness, and deceit. The family is thus a relatively efficient learning system for the development of mind, spirit, and body. It involves
the whole self. ...

Substitute the word company for family in the previous paragraph and you
get an idea of what I envision a company community to include.[23]

Another and poignant illustration of the centrality and power of family in thinking about business comes from J. Robert Ouimet of Ouimet-Cordon Bleu-Tomasso Companies on the occasion of meeting Mother Theresa of Kolkata. From this quiet and diminutive nun he learned that what he must do in his business cannot be separated from what he must do in his marriage and family. Business, he learned, is an enlargement of the circle of love:

> I simply said to Mother Teresa: "I have one question to ask you. Should I give everything I have, Mother?"
>
> She answered me clearly: "You can't give anything away. Nothing belongs to you. It has only been loaned to you. However if you wish it, you can try to manage what the Lord has loaned to you…in His way…with Him. And if you attempt to do that, you will have to follow His order in your own life, an order where Love comes first. You're married; I am not. If you want to follow His hierarchy of Love, you must start with your married life and manage what He has loaned to you. You must place your wife as your first priority. She doesn't belong to you; she's been loaned to you by the Lord. And after your wife come your four children; they don't belong to you either, just loaned to you. And after your four children come the men and women you work with. They too are loaned to you, and you will have to account for them!"
>
> She never spoke about the community, the city or the country, but only about 'the men and women you work with'…
>
> And slowly, very slowly, Mother Teresa added, "You enlarge the circle of Love because the further you go, the easier it is to love."[24]

For Ouimet, Mother Theresa's words were a revolution in the etymological sense—a turnaround of his point of view that entailed a radical change in priorities. Now he was to begin his thinking about business with his wife, then with his children, and then with the men and women he worked with. All of this in the name of one imperative—Christ's hierarchy of Love, a spiritual hierarchy beyond the world, rooted in the nuptial bond.

The Supreme Good Is Myriad

A third point to emphasize about our supreme good of being in God is that we must be open to the myriad ways that He is with us. We must know God as fully as we can so that we can be in God as fully as we can. Each of our Christian business leaders finds God in his own way. For Max De Pree at Herman-Miller, Inc., God is in the moral purpose of his business:

> This is the way I as a Christian see moral purpose—as a sign of God's presence in our organizations. It's up to us to keep the signs of moral purpose alive and visible in organizations. … Let me propose five signs of moral purpose I've seen over the years. The first sign of what I call God's presence is a wholehearted acceptance of human authenticity. … We are genuinely insiders in this world because we are God's mix—we are made in His image. Authen-

ticity needs to dominate our relationships and our understanding of justice. The implications of this belief are enormous. Second, because we are authentic, we are entitled to certain rights as insiders: the right to belong, the right to ownership, the right to opportunity, the right to a covenantal relationship, the right to inclusive organizations. ... Third, leaders in groups with a clear moral purpose make themselves vulnerable—a gift of all true leaders to their followers. ... They are strong enough to abandon themselves to the strengths of others. Fourth, groups with a clear moral purpose to their actions take very seriously realistic and equitable distribution of results. ... The fifth sign of God's presence I'd like to suggest is personal restraint. [25]

For Tom Chappell of Tom's of Maine, God is an "invisible partner" who works on his behalf to feed him new entrepreneurial ideas and to support him in their development and marketing. God, he believes, is one with him in the collective being he defines as *intuition*:

> In my opinion, intuition is something outside time and space. It is my connection to the greater human spirit, the collective consciousness of the human species—my bond, if you will, to God. [26]

And for Dennis Bakke at AES Corporation, God is in the joy workers find in their work:

> Joy at work is possible if we invest our talents as God intended. In that way we honor God and can experience His joy. The Olympic runner Eric Liddell expressed it well in the movie Chariots of Fire when we said, "When I run, I feel His pleasure." [27]

That work in business is of and for God in these and other ways has several implications. One is that it may be more than a metaphor to think of our doings at work as we might of our doings in Church; as opportunities for prayer, worship and sacrament. In business, as in religion particularly and in life generally, everything we do can and should be for God, a fulfillment of His will. Another implication is that insofar as our every act is potentially a means to the end of God, it may be a mistake to regard any of our acts as an end unto itself, as a thing to value for its own sake. This is the danger that haunts our every act—including even those of religious practice which become ends when regarded as a chore or obligation or appearance to keep up before others. To have life we must be in God and to be in God we cannot be anywhere else. Yet another implication is that while every act can and should be for God, we cannot assume that any act suffices to bring us to God. No matter how piously we act, no matter how earnestly we seek grace in every step, no matter whether we are the obedient stay-at-home son or the wayward prodigal son, our being in God is an unmerited blessing that comes only by His gift.

The Supreme Good Is Supreme

A last but not least point to emphasize about our supreme good of being in God is that it is "supreme." It is to put before and above all others and all others are to be subordinated to it. In other words, there is an order to our goods that must be lived if they are to be goods. When the good of God is foremost then all is well in our lives; then all our goods have their true meaning and place; then we are fully human. However, when the good of God slips from its rightful place—if it is denied or ignored or regarded as second to some other good—then we not only lose the good of God, we lose all of our other goods besides. Once again, as so often the case, C.S. Lewis makes this crucial point memorably and better than most:

> The longer I looked into it the more I came to suspect that I was perceiving a universal law. *On cause mieux quand on ne dit pas Causons* ['One converses better when one does not say "Let us converse"']. The woman who makes a dog the centre of her life loses, in the end, not only her human usefulness and dignity but even the proper pleasure of dog-keeping. The man who makes alcohol his chief good loses not only his job but his palate and all power of enjoying the earlier (and only pleasurable) levels of intoxication. It is a glorious thing to feel for a moment or two that the whole meaning of the universe is summed up in one woman—glorious so long as other duties and pleasures keep tearing you away from her. But clear the decks and so arrange your life ... that you have nothing to do but contemplate her, and what happens? Of course this law has been discovered before, but it will stand re-discovery. It may be stated as follows: every preference of a small good to a great, or a partial good to a total good, involves the loss of the small or partial good for which the sacrifice was made.
>
> You can't get second things by putting them first, you can get second things only by putting first things first. From which it would follow that the question, 'What things are first?' is of concern not only to philosophers but to everyone.[28]

For our business leaders the ordering of goods means that the question of what is the greatest good must be called and we cannot be indifferent to its answer. This is a point emphasized by Dennis Bakke of the AES Corporation:

> "Hey Dennis, our organization has values too," was a comment I sometimes heard from people outside our company. It was a helpful reminder that we were sometimes perceived as arrogant or even sanctimonious. Every person and every organization has values. But in this age of "tolerance," it is politically incorrect to say that any of these values is more appropriate than others. The truth, however, is that some values are better than others. Truthfulness and selflessness, for example, are preferable to deception and selfishness.[29]

Now, as it is certain that there is no good greater than God, it follows that the worldly idea that the good is for "the market" to decide could take root and flourish only in a world that has "forgotten" God, or that has "demoted" Him to the status of one good among many (perhaps as the good to seek on a Sabbath day while the others are to seek all the other days). The ethical bankruptcy of this idea shows in the moral chaos it invites. Without the greatest good of God to give proportion and meaning to other goods, there is no telling whether any act or end of business is good or evil. Are the ends of efficiency, profit, market share, achievement, status, and competitive victory always goods? Are they goods when bought with the dignity of workers or gained at the expense of "externalities" such as squandered natural resources or pollution of the environment? And what of businesses that "serve" markets for prostitution, pornography, drugs, alcohol, gambling, loan-sharking, and arms dealing? Are they to regard as good because there are large and lucrative markets to support them?

The question of the order of goods comes into stark relief when one asks of the place of profit in business. Given the assumption today that the supreme good of business is the economic interest of its owners or shareholders, it comes as a surprise that our Christian business practitioners speak together in dissent. All agree that while profit certainly is a "good" of business it is only a good when it is subordinated to the good of God. According to J. Robert Ouimet, CEO of the Ouimet-Cordon Bleu-Tomasso Group, thinking about goods at work must begin with the human person and productivity and profits will follow:

> People are important, not for productivity, but because each person is intrinsically valuable and precious." Once that had been said and affirmed, productivity took care of itself; it just naturally followed. ... If the project is truly implemented, not for the goal of increasing productivity, but out of love and respect for the workers, I can guarantee that the company's competitive productivity will not be endangered. When people feel they are being treated with love and genuine respect and, at the same time, that the company is being managed in a disciplined and productive way, they give themselves wholeheartedly to their work and become more productive. ... But if improving productivity is the prime objective when implementing this kind of management system, the project is bound to fail, because then it is nothing more than manipulation and people will sense that immediately. The organization is there to serve people and not to be served by people. Work exists for people and not people for work. A person is not 'human capital' or a 'human resource.'[30]

According to Tom Chappell at Tom's of Maine:

> Once confused about my priorities, I am now very clear: The ultimate goal of business is not profit. Profit is merely a means toward the ultimate aim of affirming the health and dignity of human beings and their families, affirming

aspirations of the community, and affirm the health of the environment—the common good. ... The world has changed. So must business. We must create a new kind of capitalism—with a heart and a soul.[31]

According to Dennis Bakke at AES:

The principles and purposes that I espouse are meant to be ends in and of themselves, not techniques to create value for shareholders or to reach other financial goals. ... Winning, especially winning financially, is a second-order goal at best. Working according to certain timeless, true, and transcendent values and principles should be our ambition. A major point of this book is to suggest a broader definition of organizational performance and success, one that gives high priority to a workplace that is filled with joy for ordinary working people. Such a place gives all workers an opportunity to make important decisions and take significant actions using their gifts and skills to the utmost. Our experience at AES showed that this kind of workplace can be the cornerstone of an organization that is vibrant and economically robust.[32]

And according to C. William Pollard at ServiceMaster Corporation:

Profit is for us a means goal, not an end goal. "What does it profit a man if he gains the whole world but loses his own soul?" the accumulation of profits in the hands of a few is never justified. Marion Wade, our founder, used to remind us, "Money is like manure. It doesn't smell any better the more you pile it up." If we focused exclusively on profit, we would be a firm that had failed to nurture its soul. ... What is there in common between God and profit? I believe there is a link. Profit is a means in God's world to be used and invested, not an end to be worshipped. Profit is a legitimate measure of the value of our effort. It is an essential source of capital. It is a requirement for survival of the individual, the family unit, and any organization of society ...[33]

Thus business is not to see as the usury of profit-seeking owners but as the means by which persons can take part in the kingdom of God. To put profit before persons is to denigrate the latter as means to an end. Profit, correctly understood, is a means to judge the health of a business, and particularly to judge how well it husbands its resources. It is not who we are but is a fruit by which we may be judged. As Christ proclaimed in the "Parable of the Talents," we are to judge by what we return to God with the talents he has given us. The more we make of His gifts the more we are in Him. For her part the Church never tires of emphasizing and supporting our struggle for being. Here is Pope John Paul II addressing a group of Argentine entrepreneurs and business people:

However, permit me to remind you that the great concern, the great business affair that you must conduct in your life, is to conquer heaven, eternal life. The

Lord says to you: "What gain is it for a man to have won the whole world and to have lost or ruined his very self?" This reverence has to be made. ...

Never forget that the real dangers are the temptations that can lead your consciences and activity astray, namely, the insatiable thirst for profit, easy and immoral gains, waste, the temptation of power and pleasure, limitless ambitions, uncontrolled selfishness, dishonesty in business affairs, and injustice towards your workers.

Carefully watch yourselves for these snares. Never kneel before the gold calf! Never abandon the narrow path of business integrity, which alone, together with a worthily earned material well-being, can offer peace and serenity to you and your families. [34]

Thus our second admonition to leaders "to put first things first" is at last an act of faith; an act in hope that by renouncing the self and the goods of worldly life one might come into being in God. That such hope is well-founded and well-funded is to see plainly in the lives of the saints in whose implacable joy we can behold the beatitude that God promises to all. And just as saintliness in Roman times won many pragmatic worldly pagans to the cause of Christ, perhaps in our times it can win many pragmatic worldly business people to the same cause.

MINISTER TO WHAT YOU CANNOT MANAGE

If, as we've said, the leader must behold in workers the Divine that he cannot see; and if, as we've said, the leader must help workers to that being that comes only by gift from God; then, with these most important things outside his control, the leader is in no position to make these things happen. Rather, the best he can do is to serve—in humility and as best he can—the God who gives life to all men. His "leading" therefore must be more ministry than management. Its gerunds must be such as "tending," "nurturing," and "empowering," rather than "measuring," "commanding," and "controlling."

And so let us ask the practical question: "What does it take to lead a business to God, so that its people (employees and customers) have more of Him, so that they have more of the life and being that He destined for them?" And let us hasten to qualify our answer even before giving it, to acknowledge that the one, true, and final answer to this question will always be beyond us to say because the Holy Spirit that leads to God is beyond our ken. The best we can do is to suggest what business leaders might do to invite grace into their lives. Here are four suggestions:

Find Your Authority in God

The business leader must know where his authority comes from and what it is for. He must understand that it comes from God and that it is for extending

His creative will on earth. Authority is a theological idea—an idea about God—that derives from the Latin *auctoritas* ("authorship") and *augere* ("augmentation").[35] It augments the authorship of society that is originally and ultimately God's. Man's authority begins in God's love, with his relinquishing to human kind some of His creative power. Man's authority thus is held in fief and founded in obedience to God, as theologian Romano Guardini neatly explains:

> Man's natural God-likeness consists in this capacity for power, in his ability to use it and in his resultant lordship. Herein lies the essential vocation and worth of human existence. . . . Only when these facts have been accepted, does the phenomenon of power receive its full weight, its greatness, as well as its earnestness, which is grounded in responsibility. If human power and the lordship which stems from it are rooted in man's likeness to God, then power is not Man's in his own right, autonomously, but only as a loan, in fief. Man is lord by the grace of God, and he must exercise his dominion responsibly, for he is answerable for it to him who is Lord by essence. Thus sovereignty becomes obedience, service.[36]

J. Robert Ouimet, CEO of the Ouimet-Cordon Bleu-Tomasso Companies sees this plainly. Inspired by his Catholic faith he seeks to lead an organization that is faithful to the social doctrine of the Church. He knows that all good is from God and that to God goes all glory:

> If there is something beautiful in my life, it must be said that it doesn't come from me, but from Him, God the Father, Son and Spirit. I've lived my life with Him because that's what I wanted and He accepted. I know my limits and my weaknesses ... I'd like to say clearly and with all the strength and conviction that I can muster: it's terribly, terribly, terribly difficult! I'd even say terrifying. If I did not have the strength of the Eucharist and the comfort from the sacrament of reconciliation, I would have probably abandoned the project long ago.[37]

The idea that authority is not for the leader's sake but for God's sake is widely shared by our exemplary leaders. For Tom Chappell of Tom's of Maine, God wills that the unique gifts of each person be incorporated in a living whole:

> Like most businessmen...I believed that authority and power are synonymous. I often wielded my power to prove my authority, and my employees quaked in their boots, appropriately intimidated...Then I reread Saint Paul's Letter to the Corinthians and was struck by what he said in Chapter 12 about the various gifts people have. "There are varieties of gifts," Paul pointed out, "But the same Spirit." I began to see how we could be different individuals but part of the same common spirit, or company; our "varieties of gifts" could be assembled in some profitable way. Later in the same chapter Paul compared the

Christian community to a "body"—"Just as the body is one and has many members, and all the members of the body, though many, are one. ... For the body does not consist of one member but of man." Though different, one body part is as valuable as the other, and all of the parts have to function interdependently to make up a complete body. Just like a successful company—one company, comprising many different parts, and gifts.[38]

For Dennis Bakke of the AES Corporation, God wills joy at work:

...God intended that the workplace be beautiful, exciting, and satisfying. Work was to be filled with joy. Work was a major reason for our creation. It was intended to be an important act of worship. It was one of the most significant ways in which we could honor our Creator. From this perspective it is our responsibility to do whatever we can to make the modern workplace the way it was intended to be. While I realize the world is not the Garden of Eden, I do believe it is incumbent on those of us in leadership roles to do whatever we can to make the workplace as fun and successful as we can.[39]

And for C. William Pollard of the ServiceMaster Corporation, God wills the dignity of each and every person:

At ServiceMaster, we have chosen to build our objectives on the conclusion that we live in God's world, and that every individual has been created in God's image with dignity and worth. It is where we begin as we try to determine the right way to run our business. ... We do not use our first objective as a basis for exclusion of people who don't believe in God. It is, instead, the reason for our acceptance of the many differences among people. Because of our starting point, we have a view—a value system if you will—that influences how we seek to operate our business, how we treat our employees, and how we serve our customers. The validity of this ethic should be measured not by what we say, but by what we do.[40]

Thus the business leader has genuine authority over others at work insofar as he acts according to God's will; as God's will is inscribed upon the moral conscience, as God's will is revealed by the moral laws of sacred scripture, and as God's will is promulgated by the teachings of the Church. To exercise authority truly is to follow His will faithfully—as scripture commends, "Thy will be done on earth as it is in Heaven."

See Your Authority as Ministry

Authority in fief is responsible authority; authority that answers God's will set forth in the Ten Commandments he gave Moses and the two-fold commandment of love He spoke as Jesus "to love the Lord God with all one's mind, heart, and soul and to love thy neighbor as thyself." These are not, as is so often complained, oppressive edicts to hamper our fun, but laws of spirit

to foster our growth in being. The reason to follow the Ten Commandments—to have no other gods, to not worship false idols, to not take the
Lord's name in vain, to remember the Sabbath day, to honor father and
mother, to not kill, to not commit adultery, to not steal, to not bear false
witness, and to not covet—is not only to stay on God's good side; it is to
have as much life as possible. The commandments are operating instructions.
This point is crucial because it means that the good of persons and thereby
the good of a business are *not* for the leader to decide and still less for the
leader to impose. This good was decided by God who built it into the fabric
of our being. It is that potency that we are to realize with others in acts of will
faithful to God.

To be effective a business leader must answer the laws of being established by God. His main concern cannot be a worldly one to make a profit or
a name. It must be to work for the community of persons that comprises his
business. This is a point of emphasis for Tom Chappell of Tom's of Maine:

> Generally, people believe their worthiness stands on how great they've be-
> come, how rich or famous. But real worthiness evolves from having sacrificed
> your time, money, and talents to build up someone who's weaker than you are,
> who needs your help, who needs your money. A real business leader seeks
> worthiness among his employees. I visit my employees; I talk to them; I find
> out what's going on in their lives. I'm one of them. I stand with them.[41]

Robert Greenleaf writes about this as the servant leader's concern for
healing. He gives the example of a conference in which twelve ministers and
theologians of all faiths and twelve psychiatrists of all faiths met to discuss
the topic of 'healing.' When the conference organizer opened the conference
with the question: "We are all healers, whether we are ministers or doctors.
Why are we in this business? What is our motivation?" This diverse group, of
doctors and ministers, of Catholics, Jews, and Protestants, needed but 10
minutes of intense conversation to agree that they are in it *for their own
healing*. Greenleaf then observes:

> This is an interesting word, healing, with its meaning, 'to make whole.' The
> example above suggests that one really never makes it. It is always something
> sought. Perhaps, as with the minister and the doctor, the servant-leader might
> also acknowledge that his or her own healing is the motivation. There is
> something subtle communicated to one who is being served and led if, implicit
> in the compact between servant-leader and led, is the understanding that the
> search for wholeness is something they share.[42]

It is worth noting in Greenleaf's account that healing is as much a good
for the servant leader as for the ones he serves. In this we are reminded that

the greatest good is not the person alone, but the person in community with others.

For his part, Max De Pree of Herman Miller, Inc. speaks about the aim of healing wholeness as "transition":

> For me the idea of transition is one of the most significant ideas that we should be reflecting on today. Transition is a matter and process of becoming. Transition is a great deal more than change. It's a growing and a maturing and an understanding and wisdom-gaining process. Transition gives us the opportunity to rise above polarization. Transition is a marvelous polishing of our intellectual and spiritual and emotional faculties. It's a process of learning who we are.[43]

And he notes particularly the important role that leaders must play in the 'transition' of others: "One of the crucial tasks of leaders—and therefore one of the ends of a leader's language—is to help move groups of people, whether a family or a church or a school, in the direction of maturity as a community. That's when people have the chance to reach their potential."[44]

In Chappell, Greenleaf, and De Pree we see how leader's authority must stand in for that of the author of all creation to support His intentions for human persons in community. In a word, the leader's authority must take the form of ministry—of service to the spirits of the people of the organization. This is to recognize, again with Robert Greenleaf, that man's greatest sin is to forget that his greatest good is man himself—the community of persons.

See Your Ministry as More than Management

This image of authority as ministry is antithetical to that more familiarly evoked by words such as "boss" or "manager" which conjure an image more dictatorial or manipulative. Indeed, the etymology of the verb "to manage" traces in part to the Latin *manus*, for hand, which is closely related to the words manacle and manipulate, and in part to the French *menager*, for the skillful direction and exercise of horses. This image of management is pervasive in the annals of thinking about business and is prominent even today. J. Robert Ouimet delineates ministry from management in recalling his own leadership as one part of each. There is first economics and management:

> In the last half-century, all the major management schools have taught an integrated system of economic management tools that can, over time, increase the competitive profitability of any organization operating in a market economy, as well as improve the efficiency of one functioning outside the market economy. The main phases of this economic [system] are planning, organization, coordination, motivation, and verification. If these percepts are rigorously followed, there is a good chance that the company will experience considerable, long-term growth in efficiency and competitive profitability.[45]

Then there is a second system that sets the first in context and balances it first by ministering to the human:

> The novel and prime concept of Our Project is to complete and rebalance this faulty system with another framework that is generally neglected or ignored—the human ISMA ... This non-economic system has as its goal to steadily improve people's lives at work. It is a system that nurtures human values that are absent in most workplaces, creating a place of joy. This joy can then spread out to the workers' families. This model, which promotes the person development of employees, can work in organization or business.[46]

Ouimet's description of this second system of administration focuses on human values of dignity, freedom, peace, serenity, humility, authenticity, brotherhood, faith, hope, and love. His idea was to create a place of joy that could not be managed top-down by imposing controls, but could only be administered by soliciting and supporting changes in the hearts of workers, changes that could come only bottom-up in the organization. Thus it was an axiom of Ouimet's leadership that it include ministerial practices and routines such as a room for silence/meditation, monthly celebrations of the Eucharist, moments of silence or prayer before and after meetings, spiritual testimonials, an annual award to celebrate caring on the job, community meals, and service the wider community. Ouimet also believed that worker participation in such should be invited but not coerced and that refusal to participate would have no career or financial repercussions whatsoever.

Management and administration are similarly delineated by Dennis Bakke of AES who describes the conventional image of "managing" (an image he traces to the industrial revolution) that must be overcome to find joy in the workplace. This image, he notes, rests on several assumptions:

- *Workers are lazy. If they are not watched, they will not work diligently.*
- *Workers work primarily for money. They will do what it takes to make as much money as possible.*
- *Workers put their own interests ahead of what is best for the organization. They are selfish.*
- *Workers perform best and are most effective if they have one simple, repeatable task to accomplish.*
- *Workers are not capable of making good decisions about important matters that affect the economic performance of the company. Bosses are good at making these decisions.*
- *Workers do not want to be responsible for their actions or for decisions that affect the performance of the organization.*
- *Workers need care and protection just as children need the care of their parents.*

- *Workers should be compensated by the hour or by the number of "pieces" produced. Bosses should be paid a salary and possibly receive bonuses and stock.*
- *Workers are like interchangeable parts of machines. One "good" worker is pretty much the same as any other "good" worker.*
- *Workers need to be told what to do, when to do it, and how to do it. Bosses need to hold them accountable.* [47]

Bakke contrasted these assumptions with those he sought to cultivate at AES. AES people:

- *Are creative, thoughtful, trustworthy adults, capable of making important decisions;*
- *Are accountable and responsible for their decisions and actions;*
- *Are fallible. We make mistakes, sometimes on purpose;*
- *Are unique;*
- *Want to use our talents and skills to make a positive contribution to the organization and the world.* [48]

"One of the most difficult lessons I have had to learn," said Bakke, "is that leadership is not about managing people. People are not resources or assets to be managed."[49]

Lead to the Beatitudes

To lead by ministry rather than management is not only to *lead from* laws of being set forth by God; it is also to *lead to* the Beatitudes identified by Jesus. Where the former establish what we must not do to not lose God, the latter establish what we must do to gain God. The Beatitudes are *the way* to be in God, *the way* to be who we are.

This perhaps is the sternest test of the business leader as it calls for faith in blessings that many regard as anything but and that few volunteer for themselves. It is to demand that the blessedness of the human spirit be held higher than worldly success. It calls the leader to unworldly ideas about worldly fortunes. Thus says the Lord, "What gain is it for a man to have won the whole world and to have lost or ruined his very self?"

An affecting lesson of the beatitudes is that what the world thinks is good may not be. Robert Greenleaf touches on this in writing of the meaning of hurt and loss in business in terms that suggest the beatitude of the "poor in spirit":

> To be on with the journey one must have an attitude toward loss and being lost, a view of oneself in which powerful symbols like burned, dissolved, broken off—however painful their impact is seen to be—do not appear as

senseless or destructive. Rather, the losses they suggest are seen as opening the way for new creative acts, for the receiving of priceless gifts. Loss, every loss one's mind can conceive of, creates a vacuum into which will come (if allowed) something new and fresh and beautiful, something unforeseen—and the greatest of these is love. The source of this attitude toward loss and being lost is faith: faith in the validity of one's own inward experience; faith in the wisdom of the great events of one's history, events in which one's potential for nobility has been tested and refined; faith in doubt; in inquiry, and in the rebirth of wisdom; faith in the possibility of achieving a measure of sainthood on this earth from which flow concerns and responsibility and a sense of rightness in all things. By these means mortals are raised above the possibility of hurt. They will suffer, but they will not be hurt because each loss grants them the opportunity to be greater than before. Loss, by itself, is not tragic. What is tragic is the failure to grasp the opportunity which loss presents. [50]

Greenleaf speaks of another beatitude; the blessedness of the meek who seek not for themselves but for others. He sees this in the love that is "unlimited liability":

Love is an indefinable term, and its manifestations are both subtle and infinite. But it begins, I believe, with one absolute condition: unlimited liability! As soon as one's liability for another is qualified to any degree, love is diminished by that much.

Institutions, as we know them, are designed to limit liability for those who serve through them. In the British tradition, corporations are not "INC" as we know them, but "LTD"—Limited. Most of the goods and services we now depend on will probably continue to be furnished by such limited liability institutions. But any human service where the one who is served should be loved in the process requires community, a face-to-face group in which the liability of each for the other and all for one is unlimited, or as close to it as it is possible to get. Trust and respect are highest in this circumstance, and an accepted ethic that gives strength to all is reinforced. Where community doesn't exist, trust, respect, and ethical behavior are difficult for the young to learn and for the old to maintain. [51]

C. William Pollard calls the leader to two further beatitudes. One is the blessedness of the merciful, of those who seek to nurture others and who gladly give without expecting to receive:

We all need to be nurtured. In the firm, it is the responsibility of leadership to see that it happens. ... we receive as we give, and in the process we understand more of what it means to be somebody. There is great potential for this to occur in our work environment, but only as the leader aligns this potential to serve with the development of the person and the mission of the firm. [52]

The other is the blessedness of the peacemakers, of those who seek reconciliation across divisions:

As I learn to be an advocate for diversity and seek to understand the differences and contributions of race, gender, and national origin, I am also learning to appreciate who people are, how they think, and what their gifts and talents are. In so doing, I am seeking to support what we all have in common, ... It is the acceptance of difference with a commitment to a common purpose and mission that allows for both homogeneity and heterogeneity. The firm then can harness the energy and creativity of difference to produce results.[53]

Pray for Guidance and Strength

To behold what he cannot see, to put first things first, and to minister to what he cannot manage (by finding his authority in God, by seeing his authority as ministry, by seeing his ministry as more than management, and by leading to the beatitudes) the business leader needs the support and sustenance that can come only by prayer, religious ritual, and the sacraments of the Church. On such supports our Christian business leaders rely, typically as a private matter at home or in Church, but in some instances as a public matter at work. J. Robert Ouimet, in particular, found prayer to be a critical element of his success: "the key to managing our organization is prayer, ever more constant in my life as CEO, as well as in that of the members of the board of directors and managers ... The whole company can be a real human community if spirituality and transcendence are integrated into its daily life."[54] This he saw as the crucial innovation of the management process he called 'Our Project': "the affirmation that, without infusing spirituality in management, it is not possible to carry out authentic human values in the business world."[55] Ouimet found wisdom in the counsel given him by Mother Theresa of Kolkata: "Do not try to manage with God without praying a lot; you won't be able to do it."[56] To meet the need for prayer in the organization Ouimet invited prayer before and after executive and board meetings, personal testaments as part of company celebrations, and a set aside a room for prayer in the company offices.

In the end, and even with the help of prayer, it is not enough for a leader to behold what he cannot see, to put first things first, and to minister to what he cannot manage. These are necessary but not sufficient conditions for good leadership. There is still to make the leap of faith. There is still the Lord's edict to leave everything of the world behind so to follow Him in faith. This is to recall the Biblical passage about the rich man who observed all of God's laws and who, when he asked Christ what he must do to enter the Kingdom of God, was saddened to learn he had to give up all that he owned to follow Christ. This was perhaps less about actually giving up worldly things than about seeing past worldly things in order to see and follow Christ truly— again, blessed are the poor in spirit. This is wisdom too for business leader who might similarly observe all of God's laws, and who has similarly to look through and beyond his worldly status and power to see and follow Christ in all that he does at work. At the end of the day there is nothing persons can do on their own to save and be saved. There is only to place themselves fully and completely in the hands of Jesus Christ who is the "one who saves."

THANKS BE TO GOD

Being is not ours to create and control, but is ours to receive and nurture. We are not God and we cannot create our being from nothing. We are children of God; persons given by Him the power of reason to know our being in Him; and a community given by Him the power to share our being in the love of one another made possible by His abiding love. In this our true meekness, we recognize God as God, as the Creator and Sustainer of all being, and we recognize ourselves as His beloved children, as those blessed by Him to take part in His Creation of all that is. This is our beatitude.

We have seen that our being at work is not an objective fact to see, but a metaphysical truth to behold. This we can do by reason and will in the image of God through the nuptial acts of love, play, and fulfillment with others. By reason we can bring the being of God to mind—in all its splendor and wonder. By will we can bring His good to our work—a good to choose according to his law. We have seen as well that God's being is available to us only as we choose it freely as our first and greatest good; as our *summum bonum*. If we do not, we cannot have it or any other good.

And so in this chapter we have been on the way to turning ourselves around by "repenting" our misconceived and misspent life at work and in business. We have been stepping back from a dehumanizing business management and stepping into a humanizing business administration. We have been finding our rest in God where in today's world we may least expect it, at work. In closing we can observe not only that God wants us to rest in Him—indeed He waits at the door waiting for us to knock—but also that He gives us the means to do so; namely, the Mystical Body of Christ that is the Church.

The Church offers clear direction for how we can be at work. And she does so by setting a clear task for any who would lead in business:

> Each of you has a vital task to carry out in the mission of the Church, a task which you carryout in the toll and labor of your ordinary working lives. Side by side with your fellow workers, you share in the creative activity of God, you forge bonds of fraternity and friendship and, like the yeast of the Gospel, in quiet but effective ways you further the Kingdom of God. [57]

Although this task has many aspects and poses many challenges to leaders it has a singular purpose, identified by Pope John XXIII as being to: "... aim that enterprise to become a community of persons in the relationships, the functions, and the position of all its subjects."[58] In discharging this task leaders can rely for help on the Church whose social doctrine: "...orients itself more towards an organization of labor and the process of industrial production which responds fully to the true dignity of the human person, the principal and irreplaceable ethical value in economic activity, since the economy and production are for the good of man and not man for the accumulation of capital."[59]

Leaders can rely upon the social doctrine of the Church because the Church is the sign and voice of the fundamental and indissoluble identity between faith and work. From the moment of creation, as noted in the book of Genesis, the experience of human work been an experience of relation to God. As John Paul II relates:

> The experience of human work—the whole experience, past and present, of human work—has its beginning in the words uttered by the Creator to the first man and woman: "Be fruitful and multiply and subdue the earth." Even though the term "work" does not appear in these words, there is a clear reference in them to the reality of work. The Creator's words establish work as the constant coefficient of human life in the prospect of earthly existence.[60]

At the same time that work binds man with the earth and its various resources, it points man to his definitive destiny of the "promised land," of God's Kingdom of Heaven. Man achieves that destiny by responding in faith to God's call to "subdue the earth," which he does through the work of his hands. And so with this observation of the power of faith to bring the peace of truth to our work lives, let us bring this book on being at work to a close with this passage from Pope John Paul II:

> These two dimensions, the dimension of work and the dimension of faith, are not two separate things, any more than the dimension of the world and the dimension of the Kingdom of God.
>
> They have been joined together in the eternal thought and will of the Creator. From the beginning, the path of faith passes through work, and the path of work through faith...
>
> So it is not true that the life of faith and hope in the Kingdom of God draw man away from work. The opposite is true: it is precisely this faith and hope that shed full light on human work, it is they that completely reveal its meaning and true value. It is the Gospel of work which fully restores his work to man. It alone enables man to realize himself as man, while with the work of his hands he transforms nature. It alone gives work its dignity. And, at the same time, the Gospel leads up to the summit of a "transfiguration" through which work shares in man's immortality, become the path to his salvation.
>
> Only when it is completely given back to man in Jesus Christ does work become a gift of God to the creature who must "subdue the earth." And at the same time man's very work is to become a dimension of that land promised to

man in God, towards which are traveling the generations of the People of God who spring from Abraham's faith.[61]

NOTES

1. Robert K. Greenleaf, *Servant Leadership* (Mahwah, NJ: Paulist Press, 1977), p. 154-155.

2. *Ibid*, pp. 159-160.

3. Frank Sheed, *Theology and Sanity* (San Francisco: Ignatius, 1993), p. 7.

4. Tom Chappell, *The Soul of a Business* (New York: Bantam Books, 1994), p. ix.

5. C.S. Lewis, "The weight of glory," *Theology, vol. XLIII* (Nov. 1941), pp. 273-274.

6. See for example, H. John Bernadin & Joyce E. A. Russell, *Human Resource Management: An Experiential Approach* (New York: McGraw-Hill, 2013).

7. Robert Greenleaf, *Servant Leadership*, p. 27.

8. C. William Pollard, *The Soul of the Firm* (Grand Rapids, MI: Zondervan, 1996), p. 129.

9. Max De Pree, *Leading without Power* (San Francisco: Jossey-Bass, 1997), p. 106.

10. For a discussion and debate of this problem see both Lloyd Sandelands, "What is so practical about theory? Lewin revisited," *Journal for the Theory of Social Behaviour, 20*, 1990, 235-262 and Robert T. Craig, "Practical theory: A reply to Sandelands," *Journal for the Theory of Social Behaviour, 26*, 1996, 65-79.

11. Michael Brown, *The Wall Street Journal* [from the late 1980's, date unknown].

12. Tom Chappell, *The Soul of a Business*, pp. 62-63.

13. *Ibid*, p. 63.

14. C. William Pollard, *The Soul of the Firm*, p. 25-26.

15. Tom Chappell, *The Soul of a Business*, pp. 141-142.

16. Viktor Frankl, http://www.youtube.com/watch?v=R_bjOeECpjI&feature=related.

17. Dennis Bakke, *Joy at Work* (Seattle, WA: PVG, 2005), p. 261.

18. *Ibid*, pp. 139-140.

19. J. Robert Ouimet, *Everything has been Loaned to You* (Montreal: To God Go Foundation, 2009), p. 91.

20. Tom Chappell, *The Soul of a Business*, pp. 114-115. This nuptial image of male and female is elaborated in Chappell's description of the company's mission statement on pp. 115-116:

The Mission Statement implies that Tom's doesn't have to be all analysis or all intuition. It can be both. We can have it all—a company that encourages the two sides of every business-person, the hard-nosed rational pursuit for more profits with the creative spirit for how to realize them. We can have a company that integrates the profit motive with the urge to do something for the community at large.

21. *Ibid*, pp. 125-126.

22. *Ibid*, p. 147.

23. *Ibid*, p. 61.

24. J. Robert Ouimet, *Everything has been Loaned to You*, p. 23.

25. Max De Pree, *Leading without Power*, pp. 179-183.

26. Tom Chappell, *The Soul of a Business*, p. 109.

27. Max De Pree, p. 260.

28. C.S. Lewis, *The Business of Heaven* (San Diego: Harcourt, 1984), p. 183.

29. Dennis Bakke, *Joy at Work*, p. 34.

30. J. Robert Ouimet, *Everything has been Loaned to You*, p. 95.

31. Tom Chappell, *The Soul of a Business*, p. 202.

32. J. Robert Ouimet, *Everything has been Loaned to You,* p. 18.

33. C. William Pollard, *The Soul of the Firm*, pp. 18-20.

34. John Paul II, *Dignity of Work*, p. 39.

35. Hannah Arendt, "What was authority?" in C.J. Friedrich (Ed.), *Authority* (Cambridge, MA: Harvard), pp. 81-112.

36. Romano Guardini, *The End of the Modern World* (Wilmington, DE: ISI, 1998), pp. 133-134.

37. J. Robert Ouimet, *Everything has been Loaned to You*, p. 90.

38. Tom Chappell, *The Soul of a Business*, pp. 133-134.

39. Dennis Bakke, *Joy at Work*, p. 74.

40. C. William Pollard, *The Soul of the Firm*, p. 52.

41. Tom Chappell, *The Soul of a Business*, p. 171.

42. Robert Greenleaf, *Servant Leadership*, p. 50.

43. Max De Pree, *Leading without Power*, p. 35.

44. J. Robert Ouimet, p. 76.

45. J Robert Ouimet, p. 69.

46. *Ibid*, p. 70.

47. Dennis Bakke, *Joy at Work*, p. 44.

48. *Ibid*, p. 72.

49. *Ibid*, p. 133.

50. Robert Greenleaf, pp. 339-340.

51. *Ibid*, p. 52.

52. C. William Pollard, *The Soul of the Firm*, pp. 47-48.

53. *Ibid*, p. 36.

54. J. Robert Ouimet, *Everything has been Loaned to You*, p. 90.

55. *Ibid*, p. 89.

56. *Ibid*, p. 127.

57. Greenleaf, p. 10.

58. Paul VI, *Gaudium et spes*, n. 78.

59. John Paul II, *Dignity of Work*, p. 17.

60. *Ibid*, p. 20.

61. *Ibid*, p. 22.

Bibliography

Aquinas, T. 1981. *Summa Theologica*, I, 93, 2, tr. Fathers of the English Dominican Province. catholicwaypublishing@outlook.com.
Arendt, H. 1958. "What was authority?" in C.J. Friedrich (ed.), *Authority*. Cambridge, MA: Harvard.
Augustine 1998. *The Confessions*, tr. M. Boulding, O.S.B.. New York: Vintage Books.
Bakke, D. 2005. *Joy at Work*. Seattle, WA: PVG.
Balbaky, E.M.L. & McCaskey. M.B. 1980. *Strike in Space*. Boston, MA: Harvard Business School, 9-481-008.
Barfield, O. 1988. *Saving the Appearances, 2e*. Middletown, CT: Wesleyan University Press.
Becker, E. 1975. *The Denial of Death*. New York: Free Press.
Benedict XVI 2009. *Caritas in Veritate*, Encyclical letter delivered July 29, 2009, #21.
Berger, T. & Luckman, T. 1966. *The Social Construction of Reality*. Garden City, NY: Anchor Books.
Bernadin, H.J. & Russell, J.E.A. 2013. *Human Resource Management: An Experiential Approach*. New York: McGraw-Hill.
Bloom, A. 1988. *The Closing of the American Mind*. New York: Simon and Schuster.
Buber, M. 1958. *I and Thou*. New York: Charles Scribner's Sons.
Burks, A.W. 1996. "Pierce's evolutionary pragmatic idealism," *Synthese, 106*(3), pp. 323-372.
Cain, S. 2012. *Quiet: The Power of Introverts in a World that Can't Stop Talking*. New York: Crown Books.
Carlson, J.W. 2008. *Understanding Our Being*. Washington, D.C.: Catholic University Press.
Cassirer, E. 1953. *Language and Myth*. New York: Dover.
Catechism of the Catholic Church, 1995. New York: Doubleday.
Chappell, T. 1994. *The Soul of a Business.* New York: Bantam Books.
Chesterton, G.K. 1959. *Orthodoxy*. New York: Image Books.
———. 1966. *Saint Thomas Aquinas: "The Dumb Ox."* New York: Doubleday.
Cooley, C.H. 1983. *Human Nature and the Social Order*. New Brunswick, NJ: Transaction.
Day, D. 2005. *Selected Writings*, ed. R. Ellsberg. Maryknoll, NY: Orbis.
DePree, M. 1997. *Leading without Power*. San Francisco: Jossey-Bass.
Emonet, P. 2000. *The Greatest Marvel of Nature*, tr. R.R. Barr. New York: Crossroad.
Feser, E. 2008. *The Last Superstition*. South Bend, IN: St. Augustine's Press.
Fisher, H.E. 1982. *The Sex Contract: Evolution of Human Behavior*. New York: William Morrow.
Freud, S. 1961. *Civilization and its Discontents*, tr. J. Strachey. New York: W.W. Norton.
Gilson, E. 1991. *The Spirit of Mediaeval Philosophy*, tr. A.H.C. Downes. Notre Dame, IN: University of Notre Dame Press.

————. 2011. *Methodical Realism*, tr. P. Trower. San Francisco: Ignatius Press.

Greenleaf, R.K. 1977. *Servant Leadership*. Mahwah, NJ: Paulist Press.

Guardini, R. 1998. *The End of the Modern World*. Wilmington, DE: ISI Press.

Hamper, B. 1991. *Rivethead*. New York: Warner Books.

Hegel, G.W.F. 1977. *The Phenomenology of Spirit*, tr. A. Miller. Oxford: Clarendon Press.

Huizinga, J. 1950. *Homo Ludens*. Boston: Beacon.

James, W. 1991. *Pragmatism*. New York: Prometheus Books.

John Paul II. 1979. Address to the Christian Union of Entrepreneurs and Managers, *L'Osservatore Romano*, 12/24/1979.

————. 1981. Laborem Exercens, http://www.vatican.va/edocs/ENG0217/_INDEX.HTM.

————. 1991. *Centesimus Annus*, http://vatican.va/holy_father/john_p.

Kreeft, P. 2012. "Happiness: Ancient and Modern Concepts of Happiness," Catholic Education Resources Council, http://www.catholiceducation.org/articles/philosophy/ph0086.htm.

Langer, S.K. 1967. *Mind: An Essay in Human Feeling*. Baltimore, MD: Johns Hopkins University.

Lewis, C.S. 1941. "The weight of glory," *Theology*, vol. *XLIII*, pp. 273-274.

————. 1984. *The Business of Heaven*. San Diego: Harcourt.

————. 1995. "De Futilitate," *Christian Reflections*, ed. W. Hooper. Grand Rapids, MI: William B. Eerdmans.

————. 2001. *The Abolition of Man*. San Francisco: Harper.

Lewis, M. 1989. *Liar's Poker*. New York: Penguin.

MacIntyre, A. 1984. *After Virtue, 2e*. Notre Dame, IN: Notre Dame University.

Maritain, J. 1966. *The Person and the Common Good*, tr. J.J. Fitzgerald. Notre Dame, IN: University of Notre Dame Press.

————. 2001. *Natural Law*. South Bend, IN: St. Augustine's Press.

Marx, K. 1972. "Economic and philosophic manuscripts of 1844," in the *Marx-Engles Reader*, ed. R. Tucker. New York: W.W. Norton.

Maurin, P. 2010. *Easy Essays*. Eugene, OR: Wipf and Stock.

Merton, T. 1979. *Love and Living*. San Diego: Harvest.

Miller, A. 1967. *Death of a Salesman*, ed. G. Weales. New York: Viking Press.

Ouimet, J.R. 2009. *Everything has been Loaned to You*. Montreal: To God Go Foundation.

Paul VI 1965. *Gaudium et Spes*, http://www.vatican.va/archive/hist_councils/ii_vatican_council/documents/vat-ii_cons_19651207_gaudium-et-spes_en.html.

Percy, W. 1983. *Lost in the Cosmos*. New York: Farrar, Straus & Giroux.

Pollard, C.W. 1996. *The Soul of the Firm*. Grand Rapids, MI: Zondervan.

Rawls, J. 1971. *A Theory of Justice*. Cambridge, MA: Harvard.

Reiner, A. 2012. "Only disconnect," *The Chronicle of Higher Education*, September 24.

Rousseau, J.J. 1950. *Discourse on the Origins and Foundations of Inequality*. Boston: Harvard University.

Sandelands, L.E. 1990. "What is so practical about theory: Lewin revisited," *Journal for the Theory of Social Behaviour, 20*(3), pp. 357-379.

————. 2001. *Male and Female in Social Life*. New Brunswick, NJ: Transaction.

————. 2005. *Man and Nature in God*. New Brunswick, NJ: Transaction.

————. 2012. *The Nuptial Mind*. Lanham, MD: University Press of America.

Schachtel, E.G. 1961. "On alienated concepts of identity," *American Journal of Psychoanalysis*, *41*(2), pp. 120-127.

Scruton, R. 2010. "Hiding behind the screen," *The New Atlantis*, http://www.thenewatlantis.com/.

————. 2012. *The Face of God*. London: Continuum.

Sheed, F. 1993. *Theology and Sanity*. San Francisco: Ignatius Press.

Smuts, B. 1985. *Sex and Friendship in Baboons*. New York: Aldine de Gruyter.

Stern, K. 1965. *The Flight from Woman*. St. Paul, MN: Paragon House.

Tablan, F. 2012. "Human alienation and fulfillment in work: Insights from the Catholic social teachings," *Journal of Religion and Business Ethics*, http://via.library.depaul.edu/jrbe/vol3/iss5.

Taylor, F. 1947. *Scientific Management*. New York: Harper & Row.

Trist, E. & Bamforth, W. 1951. "Some social and psychological consequences of the long wall method of coal-getting," *Human Relations, 4*, pp. 3-38.

Turkle, S. 2012. *Alone Together: Why We Expect More from Technology and Less from Each Other*. New York: Basic Books.

Wallace, D.F. 2005. This is Water, Commence speech to Kenyon College, 2005, Gamier, OH; http://www.yhoutube.com/watch?v=M5THXa.

Wishloff, J. 2011. "The hard truth of the Easy Essays: The crisis of modernity and the social vision of Peter Maurin," *Journal of Religion and Business Ethics, 2*(2), http://via.library.depaul.edu/jrbe/vol2/iss2/2.